MASTERING THE MOMENTS

MASTERING

A JOURNEY OF ENDINGS,

THE

BEGINNINGS, AND

MOMENTS

THE SPACE IN BETWEEN

SHAWN ELLIS

LITTLE TRACTOR
PUBLISHING

**For supporting resources or to book an event
with Shawn Ellis visit www.shawnellis.com.**

First published by Little Tractor Publishing 2024.

Paperback ISBN: 979-8-9910275-8-8

eBook ISBN: 979-8-9910275-2-6

To My Little Guru—
my son, Brody

May we exist like a lotus,
At home in the muddy water.
Thus we bow to life as it is.

Zen

Contents

Introduction

Tell me, what is it you plan to do
with your one wild and precious life?
—Mary Oliver, The Summer Day

Everything can change in a moment.

For a long time, I pointed to a moment in 2011 where my life changed—when, sitting on the floor of my home office, the phrase "this moment matters" came to me.

Then I realized the key turning point was actually on New Year's Eve in 2008, when I wrote in my journal, "Next year must be a defining year…" In other words, "this must change, now."

Upon further reflection, though, I identified another moment, in 2010, as the one that truly changed everything. It was the most unsuspecting of moments. If it stood in a line-up, you would never identify it. But while I can remember nothing else about this day, I will never forget this moment.

Picture this: A nondescript baby's room with a hand-me-down rocking chair, crib, and a simple, white folding table used as a changing table. The walls were bare. On top of the table was a fuzzy green changing pad, and on that pad laid my son, just a few months old.

This was the life-changing moment. A diaper change.

Looking into my son's sparkling brown eyes and wispy black hair—not yet as curly as it is today—a thought entered my mind: *One day I'm going to have to explain to him what I do.* At the time, I was almost seven years into owning my own business, a firm called The Speakers Group which books speakers for meetings and conferences while also offering strategic support for speakers, authors, and thought leaders seeking to build or grow their businesses. It was a business I had started, yet one I wasn't truly happy with.

Frankly, at that time, I really wasn't happy with much in my life.

Just a couple of years before, I had written in my journal, while watching *Dead Poets Society*, that, "I feel empty. Depressed. Disappointed. Lost. What is my purpose? Seize the day—my days count for nothing."

This was my response to Mr. Keating, played by the brilliant Robin Williams, who was inspiring a group of young men to live their best lives. Listening to him, taking inventory of my own life, I continued writing, "My life feels dry. Boring. Lifeless. I'm so tired of it. Where is it going?"

I was nearly a decade into an unhealthy marriage. I was unfulfilled in my work. The Great Recession was looming. I was great at dreaming big dreams, but it felt like every pursuit ended in disappointment.

"I long for heaven," I wrote. "I can't help but long for it. My life here is disappointment. Why, then, would I cherish it? No. It could not end soon enough, if heaven awaits."

That was me in 2008, and then two years later, not much had changed—except now I was the father of this amazing baby boy. And changing this baby's diaper gave me a "spark" that would set my life on an entirely different trajectory.

This was the first of many lessons Brody would teach me about living fully, which is why I've come to refer to him as "My Little Guru." I call him a guru not only because of the wisdom and perspective he has brought to my life, but also because, like any great guru, the lessons have often been quite challenging and uncomfortable. And yet, I wouldn't trade them for anything.

While changing Brody's diaper that day, not only did I think, *I'm going to have to explain to him what I do*, but *I want to be able to tell him that I do more than process contracts and payments.*

That's an oversimplified description of the work that I was doing with The Speakers Group at the time. There's nothing at all wrong with that work, but I knew I was *capable* of more, *called* to more.

Later in that same journal entry in August 2008, I wrote, "I care about people. I want to see them be the best they can be. I want to see them happy. I want to see them find and live in their strengths."

As I read it now, and reflect on that question, "What is my purpose?" it's quite clear that I knew exactly what it was. It wasn't a lack of purpose that was causing me trouble. It was fear and doubt that had been holding me back.

And that day, standing over Brody, the real question was, do I want to demonstrate a life of fear and doubt and limitation to my son? Or, do I want to demonstrate a life of purpose and possibility?

It's funny how we'll settle for things for ourselves, but then step up for someone else. Have you seen this in your own life?

In any case, I finished changing Brody's diaper and went on with the day. But the truth is, life was never again the same. While I didn't know it then, this is where the journey of *Mastering the Moments* began.

This is what I call a "reboot" moment—thinking back to the old days when a computer would get so bogged down, you'd have to power down and start over. Sometimes that just meant selecting reboot from the menu—a "soft reboot." Sometimes, in really dire situations, that meant turning it off and back on again—a "hard reboot."

The moment while changing Brody's diaper is what I would call a soft reboot—where you decide, "something needs to change" and you begin taking steps to change it. There are other times—which I've experienced, and I know you have, too—where it feels like life pulls the rug out from under us. The power cord is abruptly yanked out of the wall. That's a hard reboot.

In both cases—just like in rebooting an electronic—the objective is to begin again and come back better than before, re-aligning with your ideal operating state.

At some point in the days and weeks ahead, I wrote on the whiteboard in my office, "Work I believe in." I decided the status quo was no longer good enough. It was time to make a shift. No longer was I willing to just go through the motions.

There would be many twists and turns, starts and stops, wins and losses, on the road to find and do the work that I could be proud of. And beyond work, life had plenty of surprises of its own in store. But those words reminded me every day what I was aiming for.

Today, more than a decade later, I am proud to tell Brody that I still lead The Speakers Group, but now with a deeper meaning. We connect organizations with a diverse network of speakers united by our mission to help people live better lives and build better businesses.

In addition, I can also tell Brody that I write and speak and coach others myself, helping clients navigate the complexities of life to create lives, careers, and businesses that *they* can be truly proud of.

It's been a journey of endings, beginnings, and plenty of space in between to get here, but I'm very grateful and I take none of it for granted.

If you were to ask me how I got from that space of being empty, depressed, disappointed, and lost, to where I am now, my simple answer is: one moment at a time. Every moment on the journey—pleasant and unpleasant—has led me to *where* I am, to become *who* I am (and am still becoming), and now, to *you*.

When I look back, I wonder: would any of this have happened if not for that seemingly mundane moment of changing a baby's diaper? Maybe not. In a very real way, that moment inspired me to write this book.

Then again, I would have never had that moment if not for another moment, in the parking garage under a Five Guys burger joint, where we got the call that Brody's biological mom had chosen to place her baby with us for adoption. And that moment only came after another one, in a doctor's office, when we found out that we likely wouldn't be able to have a biological child of our own.

Of course, I may have never met Brody's mom if I hadn't moved to Nashville when I was 17 years old. And I may not have moved to Nashville if I hadn't gone to a Sawyer Brown concert with my parents when I was nine years old. That's when I was so captivated by the keyboard player that I decided I wanted to play piano—and later, to move to Music City, USA with a dream to start a band of my own.

Life is a series of endings and beginnings—"reboots"—and an accumulation of many moments in between, each shaping the next. You can't pull out one without linking it back to another. And what's really wild is that in the midst of it all, you rarely, if ever, know what's unfolding.

You've experienced this, too, haven't you? If this were only my experience, there would be no need to write a book about it. But experience tells me that when I share *my* story, you will also find *your* story. And in our stories, we find true connection. We realize we are not alone.

Can't you also point to some seemingly ordinary, routine, *mundane* moments that you would now count as *defining* "reboot" moments in your life?

And I also know there are other much heavier moments that have truly rocked your world. Some are downright tragic. The diagnosis you didn't see coming. The call you never imagined you would receive. The event that is unspeakable.

When reflecting on the moments that have truly shaped our lives, what I've learned is that it's not the circumstances themselves that have the biggest impact, but how we respond to them.

Or said another way: **Our lives are not defined by the moments that shape us, but by how we shape the moments.**

Committing to—and learning to—be more intentional about how we shape our moments as we navigate through this wild, beautiful, and sometimes heartbreaking journey called life is incredibly powerful. *Mastering the Moments* is the surest way to find more peace, joy, and meaning amidst it all. Not only for us but for those we care about and, ultimately, for the world.

As the pace of life and work accelerates and the world becomes more complex, there is a call, a cry, a demand to return to simplicity. Overwhelm and anxiety are common companions in this fast-paced world, aren't they?

With so much out of our control, when, on most days when I don't know how I'll get through it all, I remind myself of what I do know: one moment at a time. Much like atoms are the building blocks of matter, moments are the building blocks of life.

Mastering the Moments is not only a way to rise above the challenges of the day, but it's also a way to create a life that is fulfilling to you in the process. And a way to make your son proud.

One day, Brody walked into my office and said, "Hey Dad, I saw your speaking video on YouTube." *Cool*, I thought. "I left a comment." *Uh oh.*

Sure that it was going to be something about poop or other "boy humor," I immediately went to check and see what kind of disaster control was needed. My heart melted when I saw what he wrote:

"I love you dad from Brody to shawn Ellis"

No punctuation. Inconsistent capitalization. Pure and unpolished, it wasn't the comment I was *looking for* on my professional video created to win over prospective clients. However, no client comment will ever top it.

In the pages ahead, I invite you to join me on a journey through the meaningful moments that have shaped my life over the past 15 years. Some are funny, some are embarrassing, some are heartbreaking. What has defined my life, though, are the lessons I've learned through those moments.

This book is not just about my story, but it's also about supporting you in continuing to write yours. In the pages ahead, I believe wholeheartedly that you will find something that speaks to you right where you are on your own journey right now.

Whatever your stage in life, profession, or present circumstances, *Mastering the Moments* provides a roadmap for embracing life's disruptions and challenges and coming out on the other side better than ever. While the ideas will spark change immediately, practicing them will transform your life permanently.

At any moment, you can "reboot" and begin again.

So, shall we continue? If you're ready, then let's go to the end.

Chapter 1

Endings, Beginnings, and the Space in Between

Is This the End or the Beginning?

THE YEAR WAS 2019. It was a sunny day in Los Angeles, and I was on a mission. I was taking my son, Brody—aka My Little Guru—to the beach. Not just any beach, but we were returning to the very first beach he had been to as a baby.

Now, at nine years old, Brody was more interested in swinging on the bars at Muscle Beach and dropping in at Venice Beach Skatepark than playing in the sand, but I was excited to recreate this nostalgic moment. With bucket, shovel, and rake in hand, we were on our way.

We were enjoying a lovely walk, navigating the side streets from our condo to the beach, when our journey was suddenly blocked by a large yellow sign that simply read, END.

End?! What do you mean, END? The beach is right there.

Truly, it was a rather stark and humorous contrast: this bold, ominous sign dwarfed by the wide, sandy beach, the endless Pacific Ocean, clear blue skies, and palm trees just beyond it. *It looks more like a beginning to me*, I thought.

And there's a perfect picture of how, while our lives are *shaped* by moments that happen to us, our lives are *defined* by how we shape the moments.

No doubt, plenty of people have walked by that sign and thought nothing of it. No doubt, plenty of people have walked by that sign without even noticing its presence. But, for me, it's an experience I've reflected on and shared with my keynote audiences many times since. It's just so rich.

Had I come upon this sign just a couple of years before—or even a year before—I doubt I would have thought about a new beginning. That's because at that time, I was much better acquainted with endings.

I had seen my childhood dreams of being a country music star dashed. I had seen my business come crashing down in the Great Recession. I had seen a 17-year marriage end in divorce. I had nearly given up on the idea that my life would ever be what I had imagined it to be. It seemed that there was just one obstacle after another.

Almost exactly a year before looking up at that sign, I was sitting in a courtroom declaring bankruptcy. That definitely felt like an END.

Had I come upon this sign in those days, I might have just thought, *Well, if this is the end, at least it comes with a great view.* A better view than any of the other endings I had experienced.

More likely, my response would have been more cynical. *Sounds about right. Thanks for putting it right in my face.*

I was feeling a little more optimistic on this sun-drenched day in Los Angeles, though, because just a few months prior, I had celebrated my best year ever in 15 years in business. That celebration coming about nine months after I sat in that courtroom. So, bankrupt to best year ever in less than a year. Talk about a new beginning. It was beyond anything I had ever imagined.

As a matter of fact, this trip was an extension of that celebration. I was in Los Angeles for an event we had booked, and I decided to bring Brody out a few days early since taking him to that beach held some special meaning.

As I continued thinking about that sign, it occurred to me, *Isn't this the way it is in life?*

The endings are always well-marked and easy to see. You can't miss them. The end of a relationship. The end of a job. The end of a particular season of life. Sometimes the end comes by choice. Sometimes the end is imposed upon us.

"Reboot."

The new beginning, though? Not so easy to see... as we would all experience together soon enough.

Almost exactly a year after I encountered the END sign, the global pandemic turned all our lives upside down in one way or another. At the very least, we all experienced the ending of a way of life that was familiar to us. For some of us, the experience was even more traumatic.

Not only did my "best year ever" quickly fade into the rearview—a business built upon live, in-person events with large gatherings of people does not do well when you can no longer have live, in-person events with large gatherings of people—but more tragically, I lost some dear friends and loved ones. Friends lost partners and children. Perhaps you did, too. Life has never been the same.

And yet the truth is, every ending *eventually* gives way to a new beginning. It's just that unlike that day at the beach, there's not always a sandy beach, blue skies, and endless ocean staring you in the face. As a matter of fact, the new beginnings are often hidden, waiting to be discovered.

Look at your own story. While, no doubt, you've experienced *an* ending—or *some* endings—in life, it hasn't been *the* end. The fact you're still here proves that it's true, too. As long as you're still breathing, then your story is still being written.

Even if all the signs in your life right now say END—personally or professionally—you can allow those signs to define your experience, or you can open to the possibility of new beginnings. The choice, always, is yours.

Let's not gloss over the truth, though. Endings can be—and often are—painful. They are disorienting. Discouraging. Depressing, even. While it's easy to say all endings give way to new beginnings—and it's true—it is a process to get there.

Sometimes you go from an ending to a new beginning in nine months, as in my "bankrupt to best year ever" experience. Sometimes you go from an ending to a new beginning in 90 days, as I experienced in the years after the pandemic, when I was burned out on virtual events and thought I might have reached the end of my speaking endeavors. Then, I was invigorated by a vision for a new presentation titled "Beyond Resilience" and things took off again.

Sometimes, though, it takes a decade or more to find that new beginning. In reality, my "breakthrough" in 2018 was the culmination of the previous 10 years of disappointment and heartache. In the introduction, I told you about where I was in 2008—lost, empty, depressed. At the end of 2018, as the "best year ever" was secured, I wrote something very different in my journal:

"How grateful I am... just because."

Yes, I was grateful for the financial turnaround, but there was much more. I knew that the money could go just as quickly as it had come. I wasn't just grateful for a transient "good day" or "good year," but for things that could never be taken away from me. If you turn back a few months in my journal, what you'll see is that I was truly grateful for was what I had learned about life and about myself. I was grateful for who I had become. Life has never been the same.

That's why, while the sign said END, I said to myself, *it looks like a new beginning to me.*

And my hope in writing this book is that *this* can be a new beginning for you—or, at the very least, that this can be another step toward a new beginning. Whether it's within sight or not, the only way to get there is... one moment at a time. You don't have to know how everything will unfold—you rarely, if ever, will.

I can assure you, I never thought, when I moved to Nashville to pursue a career in music, that one day I would make a living taking the stage with PowerPoint rather than a piano. Or that I would write a book. Or if I did, that it would begin with a story of me staring at an END sign. And yet, here we are.

But, let's pause the talk of endings and beginnings for a moment, because the truth is, there's much more to life than endings and beginnings. As a matter of fact, most of our lives—and our moments—happen in the space in between.

This is where the work—and the magic—of Mastering the Moments truly begins.

Welcome to the Liminal Space

When I think of stepping fully into a new beginning, I think of being in flow, thriving, flourishing. It feels good. When you arrive at an ending, of course, it feels like quite the opposite. Understandably.

If only we could just flip the switch—"reboot!"—and jump straight from that yucky space into the excitement and joy of a new beginning. As much as we would like that, it's just not healthy. There is a space in between, for good reason.

It's called the liminal space. And perhaps that's where you are right now. Neither where you started nor where you're going, but rather... in between.

Liminal comes from the Latin root, "limen," which means "threshold."

I love that visual. Positioned in between the origin and the destination, it is a necessary part of the journey. Something you pass through before entering the space you desire to be in. In this space you can prepare for what is coming next, or you can gather yourself after what happened just before.

Architecture is full of liminal spaces—hallways, foyers, waiting rooms, even parking lots. These spaces are rarely—if ever—a chosen destination, yet they are valuable in helping us transition from where we started to where we're going.

Still, we typically want to move through them as quickly as possible. Just think, we curse waiting in a waiting room, even though its very name is telling us exactly what we're going to do there!

But there is often beauty to be found in the liminal spaces. If we're open to it.

Years ago, I heard about an experiment conducted by *The Washington Post* in the quintessential liminal space—a subway station—that really drove home this truth. Few people set out to just "hang out" in a subway station, but on one particular day, a man named Joshua Bell did.

If you don't know him by name, Bell is a world class, classical violinist. In this experiment, *The Washington Post* asked him to set up in a Washington, DC, subway station during Friday morning rush hour, "disguised" as a street performer. The experiment: Would anyone notice?

Bell is obviously not your average street performer. Three days before, he had sold out Boston's symphony hall, where the "decent" seats went for about $100 each. Now here he is in a subway station.

He set up and played for just under 45 minutes. In that time, he got through six well-known classical pieces and over a thousand people passed by. How many people do you think recognized him? How many people do you think actually stopped to listen for a minute or more?

Here are the answers: one and seven. One person recognized Bell. Seven people paused to listen for more than 60 seconds.

All passersby had access to a free concert that other people would pay—and had paid—lots of money for. But in the subway, who's looking for a free concert? Street performers, talented as they are, blend into the background just like the hum of your air conditioner. Everyone is just trying to get where they're going.

Here's the thing, though: We spend most of our lives in the subway. Okay, not literally, but in the sense that we are often in transit from Point A to Point B—literally or metaphorically. We're neither here nor there, but in the liminal space. And just like those subway travelers on that Friday morning, if we're not careful, we will also miss the music in the midst of the mundane.

There is one demographic that never missed the music in the subway, though: *kids*. The kids never missed the music. You can watch this play out in a video on YouTube.

At one point, a mother is walking through the subway station with her young son, hand-in-hand. She's clearly in Point-A-to-Point-B mode, but this little boy hears the music. As mom is trying to quickly exit the station, her son twists around one last time to get another glance at this master at work.

Soon enough, I would get to witness something similar with my own son, and we're going to learn how to be *in* more of the moments of our lives just like these little kids. First, though, I want to properly celebrate what it takes to get *through* the liminal spaces in life. And I want to celebrate *you*.

Celebrating Survival

Like the adults rushing through the subway station, I was trying to get through the moments of my life as fast as anyone. Facing one challenge after another, I wanted to be anywhere *but* here in many moments. I just wanted to get *there*—that proverbial place where your ducks are in a row and life is good.

In the meantime, I was just surviving. Waiting to see what the moments would bring me, hoping and praying for a miraculous turnaround. In my marriage. In my business. In my life.

In 2005, I started a blog titled "Peace in the Storm," sharing Bible verses that had spoken to me, inspired me, comforted me in difficult times—along with my commentary on those verses. I just wanted to share that comfort with others.

Looking back, maybe I should have called it "Surviving the Storm," because that's really what it was all about. These were the ideas that allowed me to endure what was otherwise unendurable.

And here's the thing: In no way do I want to demonize survival. Survival is admirable. And it's a whole lot better than the alternative.

One of my favorite scenes in the movie *Dunkirk* captures this idea of survival as an admirable feat. If you haven't seen it or aren't aware, *Dunkirk* tells the story of Operation Dynamo, the amazing World War II mission to evacuate over 338,000 Allied soldiers from the beaches of Dunkirk, France, as they were surrounded by German forces. This daring escape, aided by a flotilla of civilian and military vessels, symbolizes extraordinary resilience and unity under fire.

Toward the end of the film, as the young soldiers are returning from the harrowing battle and evacuation at Dunkirk, they are met with a mix of reactions. Many feel defeated, carrying the weight of survival as if it were a small achievement, overshadowed by a sense of failure for not winning a victory.

As they disembark, they encounter a blind man who is handing out blankets to the returning troops. This man, despite his inability to see, senses their heavy hearts. "Well done, lads," he says.

One young soldier, Alex, captures the sentiment of many when he says back to the old man, "All we did was survive."

The old man's response is simple yet profound: "That's enough."

This brief exchange highlights a powerful theme—that survival, especially in such dire circumstances, is itself a significant accomplishment. It's a poignant reminder that in life, just making it through can be an act of heroism. Having "just" survived for many years of my own life, this scene moved me because it reminded me to celebrate that important victory and the strength it demonstrates.

At this point, you've survived a lot, too. That is impressive and I'm proud of you. I'm celebrating you. When is the last time you celebrated yourself? You are amazing. Truly.

And what makes you even more amazing is the fact that, after all you've been through, you still want to do more than just survive. Rightfully so. Me, too.

I don't believe any of us, deep down, want to get to the end of our lives only to say, "Well, I survived." We are created for something more.

Survival mode is okay for a season, but not for a lifetime. It took that moment of insight while standing over Brody at his changing table to wake me up to the idea that "survival is no longer enough."

I wanted to know what it feels like to *thrive*. To feel love, joy, peace, purpose, passion, abundance—and so much more. And that same baby who "woke me up" would also be the one to teach me that if you want to thrive—whatever that means to you—it would require that I stop living to get *through* the moments and start living *in* them.

Chapter 2

This Moment Matters

Are You in This Moment or Trying to Get Through This Moment?

IT WAS A WARM summer day in July. Brody and I had gone out for a bike ride on one of my favorite trails—an activity we had enjoyed together since he was about nine months old. Initially, he rode safely on a "kangaroo seat" attached to my bike. Now about two-and-a-half years old, though, Brody had upgraded to his own balance bike. He loved it!

As we were riding, we came to a bridge that crossed above a small stream. Riding across the wooden slats of the bridge created "clickety-clack" sounds and a "bumpety-bump" vibration in your seat. Both were a thrill to Brody, so I stopped and sat on a bench at one end of the bridge to let him ride his bike back and forth across it. Doing so brought the biggest smile to his face!

I've loved riding my bike since I was a child, but I don't remember the last time I had such a big smile on my face while riding. Brody's smile was so big that I took a picture with my phone, and then I had to stop him to ask, "What are you thinking about?"

I wanted to know: *What is it that is bringing you so much joy right now?*

Without hesitation, he answered, "Riding my bike."

Nothing more, nothing less.

And that's exactly the kind of lesson that led me to title him "My Little Guru." He was truly a master of the moments with his child-like awareness and curiosity—just like all those kids in the Washington, DC subway station. Probably like the kids you know.

After hearing his matter-of-fact answer, I was left thinking, *of course*. What else *would* he be thinking about?

I don't know what I expected him to say: "this morning's perfect oatmeal?" or "my amazing idea to build a tower of blocks later?" But I do know that if you were to ask me what I was thinking about while riding my bike, it probably wouldn't be *riding my bike.*

I can almost guarantee I would have told you I was thinking about something that happened in the past—probably something that I wished wouldn't have happened that way—or something coming up in the future—something that was scaring me, which likely wouldn't happen anyway. Or, if I were honest, maybe I would have told you how I was thinking about how awful my life was and how I didn't know how I was ever going to get it all turned around.

But, back to Brody. The joy expressed in his smile was undeniable. Having lived so long in survival mode, just trying to get *through* the moments, his smile gave me a picture of what joy looks like. I wanted to feel more of that in my life.

Don't we all?

Think about the wild success of *The Joy of Painting* with Bob Ross, or best-selling books like *The Joy of Cooking* by Irma Rombauer and *The Joy of Sex* by Alex Comfort. Collectively those works have reached millions. Not because millions wanted to know "how to paint" or "how to cook" or "how to do it." "How to" is easy to find. *Finding the joy* is what requires more skill—starting with this skill of being present.

As a matter of fact, that experience with Brody on his bike has inspired me to check in with myself periodically by asking one simple question:

Are you in this moment or trying to get through this moment?

With the dizzying pace of life, an overwhelming list of things to do, and one surprise after another, I often catch myself just trying to get *through* the moments. Surviving. Again.

As adults, we're often just trying to get through the moments, aren't we?

Through this meeting...

Through this day...

Through this season...

Once I get *there*—meaning, past *this*—*then* things will be good. Then, I'll be happy. Finally, I'll feel peace. But it's a trap. Because *here* is where we are, always. Even if *here* is in the liminal space.

Learning to *be* here, even when life is moving faster than we would like, when we aren't so happy about the circumstances, and when we wish things were the way they used to be, is the next step on the journey.

Living Like the Lotus Flower

Mastering the Moments isn't just about being present when things are what they want them to be. It's about actively engaging with whatever life serves us, shaping our moments with intention and purpose.

Think about the lotus flower.

This remarkable flower begins its life buried in the murky, muddy bottoms of ponds and rivers. Against all odds, it reaches upward towards the light, emerging pristine and bright above the water's surface.

Just as the lotus does not allow the mud to mar its beauty, we too can rise above our circumstances. The muddy water in our lives—our challenges and difficulties—provides the very sustenance we need to grow, to flourish, and to ultimately succeed. Embracing these challenges with grace and resilience, as the lotus does, transforms them into opportunities to bloom spectacularly.

But it does require that we develop some additional skills and practices. Ahead, let me share three that have made the biggest difference for me—and that just might do the same for you.

Slowing Down

Being *aware* of the moments is where we begin, but even with awareness, if we're always rushing through the "subway station" of life to get from Point A to Point B, we'll still miss many of the moments. We must slow down, and I think if we listen to our heart or spirit or soul, we *feel* that. But also, when our brain takes inventory of all we have to do—and all we haven't done—it says, "we can't do that."

Our brain says we must "do more, faster." The world says we must "do more, faster." *That's* the way to succeed. So, we run the race, and we wait and hope for the day when life will slow down, so then *we* can slow down.

I came across an essay by economist John Maynard Keynes titled "Economic Possibilities for our Grandchildren." Published in 1931, during the Great Depression, Keynes predicted a future where technological advancements and increased efficiency would drastically reduce the need for labor. He projected that by now—as I write—people would only need to work 15 hours a week to complete the necessary tasks and meet their needs. The rest of the time would be free for leisure.

Sounds amazing, doesn't it? Yet, many of us are more familiar with working 15-hour *days* than 15-hour *weeks*.

In terms of technological capabilities, Keynes' predictions sound reasonable. Think about the rise of AI and tools like ChatGPT, which can complete tasks in seconds that once took hours. AI alone has given us the opportunity to upgrade our efficiency like never before.

But what do we do? We fill the new gaps with something else. Like checking email while standing in line at the grocery store. (If you still go to the grocery store.) We're driven to do more, yet we keep hoping life will slow down. Quite a paradox.

The more "advances" there are to help us, the more we fill in the space created by that "help." But, if you feel like you're already moving fast—often at a frantic pace, you might say—then how is it going to feel if you keep pushing your limits, trying to do more, faster, to keep up with the accelerating pace of life and work?

Maybe you would argue that the only way to keep up is by doing more, faster. I get it, but also: Has moving faster ever allowed you to completely finish your to-do list, leaving you to think, "I wonder what I'll find to do tomorrow?"

I know I've never had that experience. But I have found myself feeling exhausted and burned out after the constant rushing and pushing and striving to get it all done. Trying to get it all done feels like playing a game of Whack-a-Mole. Even with the latest and greatest time management strategies, the to-dos keep coming.

The transformational moment came when one day, feeling totally defeated and helpless by it all, it hit me: *Wait a minute. I've never got it all done, and yet, the world is still turning. Maybe I'm putting too much pressure on myself.*

Today, I constantly remind myself, *I can only do what I can do.*

That doesn't mean life stops sending requests. That's why when the requests start stacking up, I have to say—to myself, at least—"take a number." For those of us who are achievers or pleasers, it's easy to promote every new demand for our time and attention to "right now" status. And that's when we burn out.

Instead, imagine if your calendar or to-do list had one of those red number dispensers like at delis and pharmacies. Every new request has to "take a number" and wait its turn. And you can always decide what's most important and move things around, but the key is, *you decide.*

Then, you focus on one priority at a time—do what you're doing—like Brody was focused on riding his bike, and see how your experience changes. I've found that even tasks I don't really enjoy—like bookkeeping—can become enjoyable if I'm not just cursing it and rushing to get to the next thing.

And, while we might initially think that someone or something is "losing out" by not being at the top of the list, the reality is that everyone and everything gets more of you when it *is* their turn. That person, that task, that meeting, gets your full attention, and your attention is the conduit to all you have to offer.

What would it mean if you were in conversation, and you truly *heard* what the other person was saying rather than getting bits and pieces while thinking about the next thing on your list? What if you had the space to not only hear the words, but to slow down to ask, *What do they really mean? What are the feelings behind these words?* How much more meaningful might the engagement be if you understood where they're coming from and what really matters to them? The full story is rarely told in someone's words alone, and we miss all of that if we're not really present.

Tony Schwartz runs a company called The Energy Project. He's a performance and energy specialist, and he wrote on the *Harvard Business Review* blog that "Speed is a source of stimulation and fleeting pleasure. Slowing down is a route to depth, more enduring satisfaction, and to excellence." Well said.

At some point today, I encourage you to try on one of these mantras:

I can only do what I can do.

Take a number.

Do what you're doing.

One thing you must be prepared for, though. Not only does slowing down open the door for you to experience the beauty and fullness of the moment, but also to experience something else: the pain or frustration or other unpleasantries of the moment. Sometimes, that's exactly why we're moving so fast—because we don't *want* to experience the parts of life that we don't like.

I once pointed this out during a small workshop and a woman sitting on the second row let out an audible, "Whoa!" as if she had just unlocked the key to all of life's mysteries. When you slow down, you may very well find something in this moment that you'd rather not have to acknowledge or experience. You can't fully experience joy without also being open to the pain. The life experience is *all* of it. Even so, that doesn't mean you have to *like* all of it to be *open* to all of it.

The journey of *Mastering the Moments* continues.

Allowing What Is

Seeing Brody riding his bike, with that big smile of total joy, hearing him say that all he's thinking about is "riding my bike," it's easy to say, "Of course. Easy for you, kid."

Naturally, at age two, a child doesn't have to worry about all the things we have to worry about as adults. Also, at age two, a child's brain isn't developed enough to worry about all the things we have to worry about... or to think all the thoughts we think.

If you want to experience that kind of joy, though, the truth remains: the only way to experience it is in this moment. So, how do we do that with all the complexities of life today? Living in constant uncertainty with disruption and change coming at a pace unlike anything we've ever experienced?

On one hand, we could say, "Would be nice to be a kid again," and indeed, many of us would do well to recover some of that childlike wonder and awe we once had.

I remember a time when I took Brody to a Christmas festival where they had sledding hills, train rides, hot chocolate stations, a concert, and more. As we were walking back toward the car at the end of the evening, I asked him, "Hey buddy, what was your favorite part?"

Once again, his answer floored me.

"All of it," he said.

Of course. It was *all* amazing. Sledding? Trains? Hot chocolate? Live music? What's not to like?!

Again, as adults, we often live with such a binary view. *This* is good. *This* is bad. *This* is my favorite. *This* I didn't like. We categorize everything.

For Brody and children, though? No need to pick a favorite. *All of it* was my favorite.

So, what, we should just all return to living like we were two or four again?

No. Because while that childlike wonder and awe is to be admired and even aspired to, there's also a child*ish* nature that we must learn to leave behind.

Think back to Brody on his bike.

If someone had come along and grabbed Brody's bike and thrown it over the bridge, would he have still had that smile on his face? Of course not. He would have had a complete meltdown. (His dad would have been pretty pissed, too.)

If, at that Christmas festival, Brody's hot chocolate had spilled all over the ground, would he still have loved all of it? No, he would have had a complete meltdown.

I know, because I saw plenty of times when it happened.

I remember when he was a baby, still taking his bottle, when he was hungry, you would *know* he was hungry. He was a happy baby overall but when he wanted that bottle... he wanted it *now!* And if you gave it to him two seconds past now, he would scream and let you know what a miserable job you were doing meeting his needs.

Brody's experience was totally attached to his circumstances. That's to be expected of a child. And yet, it's also not so different from how we live as adults much of the time, is it?

I remember a time when I was on my way to my Mindfulness-Based Stress Reduction (MBSR) course at Vanderbilt. It was about a 25-minute drive, and on this night, I was running late.

What inevitably happens when you're running late?

There's traffic. You hit all the red lights. All the things.

That was my experience, and I was getting anxious. I had the destination set in my GPS and the arrival time was getting later, the further I drove.

This isn't good, I thought.

I'm going to be late.

That's so disrespectful.

I'm going to walk in and disrupt the whole class.

It sounds crazy when you hear that we have tens of thousands of thoughts a day... until you start noticing your thoughts, and then you realize, *that sounds about right.*

I remembered something that we were taught on the first night of class, though. Elmo, the instructor, said one of the rules of class is to "arrive practicing."

What is mindfulness about?

Mindfulness, as defined by Jon Kabat-Zinn, creator of MBSR, is "awareness that arises through paying attention, on purpose, in the present moment, non-judgmentally."

To arrive practicing, then, is to arrive paying attention, on purpose, in the present moment, non-judgmentally.

I had a lot of judgment going on in this particular moment.

I was being childish.

This isn't how it's supposed to be.

This isn't how I want it to be.

I don't like it.

This is horrible.

And here's what I realized: none of these thoughts are going to change my arrival time. All they're doing is causing me to get more worked up. They're triggering the release of more adrenaline and more cortisol—the stress hormones—in my body. I'm getting more tense. And I'm certainly not finding any joy in this moment.

I decided to stop darting in and out of traffic, trying to pick up positions like a NASCAR driver. I decided to stop tailgating. I took a deep breath in, let it out slowly, loosened my grip on the steering wheel, and decided to just allow this moment to be what it is.

Allowing.

This is another lesson I learned from Elmo.

He made a distinction between *allowing* and *accepting* that has always stuck with me.

To *accept* this moment, which we're often taught in mindfulness, sounds quite challenging. When you're facing difficult or unpleasant circumstances, to accept them sounds like you're putting your stamp of approval on them.

It makes me think of the old days of collect phone calls.

The phone would ring, and you would hear a voice say, "I have a collect call from Jane Smith. Will you accept the charges?"

In this case, though, it's life saying, "I have some circumstances you aren't going to like. Will you accept?"

With a collect call, if you say no, that's the end. No more phone call.

In life, though, if you say no... the circumstances remain.

Then you're left with circumstances you don't like *and* the experience of resistance which might include feelings of anger, sadness, frustration, resentment, or any number of depleting emotions.

To *allow* the circumstances, though, as Elmo taught us, sounds—and feels—a lot less permanent. And, to *allow* the circumstances doesn't mean you *like* them. It just means you're not going to fight against them.

This lesson reinforced what I had recognized when the phrase "this moment matters" came to me. It's one thing to understand the importance of the moment, but now I had a tangible practice to apply it more consistently.

Elmo also gave us a mantra: "It is what it is... while it is."

I had heard "it is what it is," as I'm sure you have. It was never used in a space that felt "mindful," though. To the contrary, it has a feeling of resignation about it.

Maybe you've heard someone say, when facing undesirable circumstances, "it is what it is," followed by a quiet sigh. Rather than being mindfully engaged in the moment, this is often a statement of disengagement. It's the relinquishment of one's personal agency, not only surrendering to the circumstances but also to the feeling of frustration, helplessness, or despair. It implies a static universe where things are fixed, leaving us with no role but to accept what is served.

When you add those three simple words—"while it is"—to the common phrase, though, everything changes. Or, at least, it did for me.

While it is affirms a recognition of impermanence.

MaMa, my dad's mom, had her own version of this mantra: "This too shall pass."

Maybe you've heard that one, too. And it's true.

The only constant in life is change, and whether you say, "It is what it is while it is" or "this too shall pass," both mantras remind us that our current situation, no matter how challenging, is temporary. Rather than being resigned to reality, this perspective opens the door to engage with it actively, with the understanding that the present moment is fluid and malleable.

When I remembered to "arrive practicing" on that stressful drive to the MBSR class, I wasn't just resigning myself to the traffic and the potential tardiness. I was engaging with my current reality with intention. By shifting my focus from frustration and helplessness to observation and presence, I transformed my experience.

I turned on some music. I relaxed. I found that I actually had a few minutes to experience joy. And you know what? I arrived at class three minutes early. And that's why that experience was such a memorable one.

At that point, it hit me: *Wait.* So, I could have spent the entire drive tense, stressed, cursing my fellow drivers, and the only "loser" in that experience would have been me. I would have still arrived on time... but I would have given away what became a space to experience peace and joy.

How often do we do this in life?

Are you stressing about some circumstances in your life right now? And how is your stress impacting those circumstances? Is it doing anything to resolve them? Or is it only changing your experience?

I am very aware that if we could sit down across the table from one another, you could tell me about a lot of "stuff" going on in your life. I know there's a lot of uncertainty. Maybe your inbox is overflowing. There are probably challenges that you wouldn't even want to speak of. Plenty of reasons to be stressed.

And yet, right now, as you're reading this, are you okay? Are you safe? Are your needs met? If so, there's good news: there's only right now.

Let's see if we can deepen that feeling of being okay.

Try this:

    1. Take a deep breath in, and let it out slowly.

    2. Do that again, counting to five as you breathe in, then holding for the count of five, then exhaling to the count

of five.

3. Repeat that 5-5-5 breathing pattern three more times.

4. Continue breathing at a natural, relaxed pace, just a little slower and deeper than usual.

That last step is especially important to get maximum benefit here, as I've been reminded while coaching Brody on this very thing lately.

Given that he experiences other emotions—like frustration, anger, and anxiety—just as intensely as he was experiencing joy that day on his bike, we're trying to help him develop his own practices to find his way back to a place of calm.

A couple of days ago, on a morning when he was emotionally dysregulated and "on edge," not listening fully to anything I said but arguing with everything, I told him to take a breath. He responded—just as quickly as he told me he was thinking about riding his bike—that, "I *am* breathing! I wouldn't be here if I wasn't breathing!"

Okay, buddy, let's try this again…

It's not only important *that* you breathe, but *how* you breathe—in this case, a little slower and deeper than usual. As it turns out, this is one of your body's natural mechanisms for interrupting stress and returning to a place of calm, restoring emotional regulation.

Unlike just telling yourself or someone else to "just calm down"—which you've likely discovered is rarely, if ever effective and will most assuredly lead to eyerolls, sarcastic comments, or worse—changing your breathing works wonders. Calm will return naturally within as little as two minutes.

As someone who is still prone to be overcome by anxiety or frustration, I've found this to be tremendously helpful. I encourage you to try it, too.

When you find yourself feeling agitated, angry, or scared, for instance, recognize that your body has shifted into survival mode. In survival, your body is flooded with stress hormones like cortisol and adrenaline. Your body has sensed a threat—whether physical or psychological—and it's on guard and ready to fight.

Taking those breaths and continuing to breathe a little slower and deeper than usual signals to your body that it's safe to settle back down. Then your brain function shifts from the amygdala to the prefrontal cortex, your learning centers turn back on, and you are in a better condition to address whatever challenges are in front of you.

While it's tempting to dismiss allowing the circumstances of this moment and changing our breathing as being inactive or passive, what I've come to realize is that this is our first act of creation. No longer are our circumstances dictating our experience, but we are taking an active role in creating the experience we desire.

Yes, our ultimate desire is joy, but developing the ability to find calm in the midst of the chaos is a powerful first step. Allowing what is releases the tension between our expectations and reality. Allowing what is—while it is—opens the door to what can be. Learning how to step into it was a lesson yet to come.

But not the *next* lesson.

Letting Go

There's another key to both living fully in the present and stepping confidently into the future. That's learning to let go.

To move forward, we must detach, or untether, or let go of what was. And that's not easy. On this journey of *Mastering the Moments*, I've come to believe that life is a series of lessons in letting go. The Buddha said, "permanence is an illusion."

We come into this world grasping for something to hold on to. Have you seen the cute pictures of a tiny baby's hand gripping a parent's finger? Maybe you've experienced it firsthand. Holding on to something gives us comfort. And there's nothing wrong with wanting to hold on to something—or someone. We just have to have an awareness that everything we hold on to will eventually pass away.

Loved ones. Life stages. Clients. Pets. Neighbors. Children. All will come and go. This is the natural flow of things. Speaking of flow, look at a stream of water. This is the perfect model for life—it's always moving, and always moving forward.

That said, losing people and things we care about hurts. Sometimes, a lot. Sometimes, a seemingly unbearable amount. Pain is a normal part of the human experience, and pain is there to feel, not deny or suppress. *Suffering*, on the other hand, happens when we are out of alignment with the nature of things.

You might be expecting me to tell you another Brody story here, but the most vivid lesson I've learned about letting go comes not from My Little Guru, but from my sweet four-legged companion, Lucy.

Lucy had been with me for almost 15 years of my life when the time came to say goodbye. She was with me when I sat in my bonus room watching *Dead Poets Society*, writing in my journal about feeling empty, depressed, disappointed, and lost. She was with me when I celebrated my best year ever. She was even by my side while I was writing early drafts of this book—literally, lying next to me, using a stack of pages as her pillow.

Knowing that her end was near, I took her for a walk on a trail by the lake where we had walked together one time when she was younger. Then exactly one week later, a few days after she had died, I walked the same trail by myself, in remembrance of her, and to process the loss.

I spoke to Lucy while I walked. I told her how much I loved her and how much I missed her. And I missed her *terribly*.

As I spoke to her, though, it hit me: *I miss her, but I don't want her back.* She was in a lot of pain near the end due to a cancerous growth on her leg. She deserved rest. Plus, there was no bringing her back. To want her back would be out of alignment with the nature of things. That is when we experience true suffering.

Letting go of what was is the flipside of allowing what is. Just like resisting what is present will block you from entering the present moment, clinging to what was will block you from moving forward. The stream of life keeps moving forward and we must learn to flow with it.

Later that day, I was back home, walking through the dining room into the kitchen when I glanced out the back patio door. Something in the sky caught my eye. It was a cloud that looked like the silhouette of Lucy's head, peeking from behind some trees. Of course, you can find almost anything you want to see in a cloud formation, but this struck me because I had once taken a picture of us on that back deck, with her facing the same direction.

What was even more amazing to me was that on my walk, while talking to Lucy, I had told her that I'd love to hear from her sometime if it was possible. If she could visit me in a dream, or in the clouds, or anywhere, any way, it would be a gift. Is that what I was experiencing?

I grabbed my phone and took a picture of the cloud. Then I looked back outside a couple minutes later and the cloud had morphed into some other shape. I had to let go of that, too. But I also thought, *what if I hadn't walked through the house at that moment?* What if I hadn't looked out the window? It was as if it had taken shape right there, right then, for me to see.

But maybe I'm just crazy.

The next day, I went out to run some afternoon errands. I was driving around in silence when I decided to turn on the radio. I had been listening to the Beatles station on satellite radio when I was last in the car, so that's what was on when I turned it back on. Can you guess what song was playing? The words "Lucy in the Sky" were on the car's display screen.

It was as if to confirm, "Yes, you saw what you think you saw."

So, if you ask me, nothing is ever really gone. It just changes form. The energy of "the thing"—the person, the relationship, the job, whatever—moves elsewhere. As that energy moves elsewhere, so you must also shift your energy to keep moving.

What I've found is that, while embracing this idea doesn't alleviate the pain of loss and letting go, it does alleviate the suffering.

Here in the liminal space, not where you once were and not yet where you're going, it's natural to grieve. It's natural to need some time to rest. But when you are ready, you can rise.

Have you lost anything recently that you're struggling to let go of? It could even be the fact that life just hasn't unfolded the way you had imagined it would.

Let me share the framework for a process that I've found to be very helpful. It came to me in a moment of inspiration while dealing with another loss, and it guided my walk after Lucy had died, too. I call it Extract the Good because it's designed to help you do just that—extract the good from past experiences and let go of the rest.

Growing up on a farm, I think of a combine going through the field to harvest grains. Extracting the good is like taking the grain from the stalks of wheat, separating it and discarding the chaff. Or, to use a non-agricultural illustration, we could say, keep the gift and throw away the wrap.

Think of something in the past that has some kind of hold over you. It could be something from the past that you miss, or something from the past that you regret or resent. Here are the three steps to Extract the Good:

1. *Accept What Is:* Know, it is what it is, while it is. This is present. This is reality. Working with what is starts with accepting what is.

2. *Reflect and Remember:* Reflect on the good that remains from that relationship, person, or experience. Think of joyful moments if it was something positive. Go there. Experience those moments again. Feel those feelings. And know, this will always be with you. You can go

there anytime. If it was an unpleasant situation: What did you learn from it? What do you know now that you didn't know before? Are you stronger or wiser? Do you have a greater capacity for compassion? Can you better understand others? At the very least, can you be thankful that that moment brought you to this place, the threshold to a new beginning? Celebrate that. Take it in. That will always be with you.

3. *Release and Let Go:* Let go of the parts that no longer serve you. If it was a person or situation you loved, can you release it into the sky like a helium-filled balloon, and let it go to become whatever it desires to become? If it was something you regret, or resent, can you release it into the sky knowing that it is finished. It is in the past. It no longer exists anywhere except in your mind. Can you release it? You've extracted the good from it, so you keep the benefit. But the part of it that has been holding you down, the dead weight—because it truly is dead—can be released. Now, do you feel lighter?

Letting go of what holds you down—including resentment or attachment to the past—is as crucial as "getting fired up" when you want to rise and move forward in life. Just like a hot air balloon must untether from the ground and release extra weight to reach its highest altitude, we, too, must let go of what weighs us down to soar to our fullest potential.

Slowing down, allowing what is, and letting go of what was are powerful practices on the journey of *Mastering the Moments*. When you're using these practices, what you're really using are what I call your Three Tools of Creation. It's a shift in your attention, attitude, or action. With these three tools, you can truly change everything—about what is, and what can be.

Let's take a closer look at how they function and how you can harness their power to create a life filled with purpose, joy, and meaning.

Three Tools of Creation

If you unpack everything we've learned about *Mastering the Moments* so far, you will find that there are three foundational tools at work in any given moment: attention, attitude, and action. In any given moment, you're *focused* on something, you're *thinking* something, and you're *doing* something. And this, rather than your circumstances, is what is creating your experience.

Our task in *Mastering the Moments* is to bring more intention to what is often happening on autopilot. By mastering the use of these Three Tools of Creation we gain the power to transform our moments and, consequently, our lives.

Attention: What Are You Focused On?

Every day has the ingredients to be a good day or a bad day. What you "make" of today is totally dependent on how you look at it. You can focus your attention on everything that's going wrong at any given moment, or everything that's going right. You can focus on everything that's missing, or everything you have. You can focus on all the things you can't change, or on what you can change.

Think back to Brody on his bike. His focus was entirely on doing what he was doing. Paying attention to the present moment brought him total joy. Imagine applying that level of focus to the things that matter most to you.

To assess the role of your attention in creating your experience, consider:

- What has held your focus today?

- Does that feed joy or sadness? Confidence or worry?

- Are you focusing on what empowers you or disempowers you?

What you focus on has a direct influence on your next choice.

Attitude: What Are You Thinking?

According to The Cleveland Clinic, we have about 60,000 thoughts a day. Most of them are repetitive, and the majority of those are negative—like the limiting beliefs and stories we tell ourselves. Remember those stories I started telling myself when I got stuck in traffic on the way to my mindfulness class?

- *I'm going to be late.*

- *That's so disrespectful.*

- *I'm going to walk in and disrupt the whole class.*

I wasn't experiencing traffic, per se. None of the other cars—or drivers—were doing me any harm. What I was experiencing was the thoughts and beliefs I had because of the traffic. They're silly thoughts when you notice them and write them down. Yet they're totally normal.

The fact that we have thoughts like these is not a problem. The problem is that they often capture us unaware. With awareness, though, you can rob those stories of *their* power and start reclaiming *your* true power.

Try this periodically:

1. *Notice* the thought you're having.

2. *Consider* how that thought makes you feel, or what it makes you want to do.

3. *Choose* whether you want to hold on to that thought or let it go.

It really is as simple as that. Admittedly, though, some thoughts will try to convince you that you need to hold on to them. You've surely heard the advice, "Don't believe everything you read," or everything you hear. That's good advice. And so is this: "Don't believe everything you think!"

When you don't like how a thought is making you feel, but for whatever reason, you just can't shake it, ask yourself this question: "Are you sure?" Later, I'll tell you a story about how that one question transformed my entire approach to parenting.

Questions are powerful. Especially when you answer them honestly.

Action: What Are You Doing?

We're always doing *something*, but not always the *right* thing—in relation to what we want to experience in our lives.

Growing up in the country, I remember one entrance into my grandpa's farm. Specifically, I remember the deep ruts that had been carved there. After a heavy rain, you would want to get out of those ruts to avoid getting stuck in the mud. The challenge was that the slick, swampy mud would try to pull you right back in.

As a kid riding with Grandpa in his truck, I thought it was a lot of fun to slip and slide through this gate. But today, I think of this when considering the "swampiness" of our habits, our comfort zone, and our past experiences—all of which can easily guide our actions from moment to moment if we're unaware.

Just as following those deep ruts will always be the easiest path in the truck—you can take your hands off the wheel and the truck will practically drive itself—it's always easiest to make choices "by default" in life, too. But will that take you where you want to go?

We don't want to push or force or fight with what life puts in front of us. That's exhausting and fruitless. But we also don't want to let life just drag us along at will. That's not *Mastering the Moments*.

Up ahead, we'll talk about how to choose the "right thing, right now"—and I'll share a very practical tool to help you align your actions with your deepest desires—but for now, just notice your tendency to get stuck in the "ruts" of your old habits, patterns, and routines and see how that's shaping your life.

The "Switch" Method: Applying the Three Tools of Creation

I saw something while observing Brody at gymnastics one day that I adopted and transformed into what I call the "Switch" Method.

The coach had the kids broken up into small groups, with each group on a different apparatus. After a certain amount of time, she would yell out, "Switch!" and they would rotate to the next station. It made me think, couldn't we do the same to avoid getting "stuck" in a certain pattern of focus, thoughts, or behavior?

At any given moment, you can "switch" your attention, attitude, or action:

1. *Attention:* Notice what you're focusing on. Is it empowering or disempowering? Does it feed joy or sadness? If it's not serving you, you can "switch" your focus to something that does.

2. *Attitude:* Observe the thoughts and beliefs you're holding. Are they limiting or uplifting? If they bring you down, you can "switch" your perspective to something more positive and empowering.

3. *Action:* Evaluate what you're doing. Is it moving you toward your goals or keeping you stuck in old patterns? If it's not productive, you can "switch" your actions to align with your desired outcomes.

I've found this to be a very helpful method to reclaim your power over your experience and transform a moment, but as with everything I'm sharing with you, my suggestion is simply: give it a try.

When you notice a negative thought, habit, or pattern and you decide it's time to let it go, simply say to yourself, "Switch!" and redirect your energy toward a more positive and productive direction. By making even the subtlest shift in your attention, attitude, or action, you are living as the creator of your experience rather than just a victim of your circumstances.

And we could end the book right here.

We've explored how life is a series of endings and beginnings, much of it happening in the space in between. We know that the way to best experience all of it is to slow down, allow what is, and let go—utilizing our Three Tools of Creation.

By the time I had learned all this, I thought it was everything. *I can face any challenges and be content in all things.* Relationship challenges, parenting challenges, business challenges, you name it. *I've got this.* But I didn't "have this."

While we do have the foundation of working with what *is* at this point—and it's critical that we start there—the journey of *Mastering the Moments* is about more than working with what is. It's about seeing and stepping into what *can be.*

It's easy to slip from a state of contentment into a state of complacency, which is why we must be careful not to. Our goal is not just to find a more "elegant" version of survival mode, but to continue in pursuit of true joy, continually choosing to focus, think, and act in ways that align with our highest aspirations.

This was—and still is—the harder part of the journey for me. It's also the one that is the most rewarding. Ahead, I'll share how I discovered the specific "work I believe in" after that spark of inspiration during Brody's diaper change, and the surprising turns—and even more powerful lessons—that followed.

As always, everything can change in a moment.

Chapter 3

Live Your Calling

Desire + Decision = Change

IT WAS ALMOST A year after committing to "work I believe in"
that I was in San Diego for an association board meeting. While
I was there, I took the opportunity to connect with a few of my
speaker friends and colleagues in the area.

The first thing that struck me as we met for coffee, lunch, and
dinner was that they each pulled up in a sweet ride—Allan in
his classic Jag, Harry in his sleek Mercedes, Steve in his stylish
BMW. While I'm not a super "material" guy, I do admire nice
cars. I guess that goes back to my childhood. More on that later.

What left more of an impression on me than their vehicles,
though, was the conversation. While I had worked with some
of the world's best speakers for more than a decade at that point,
I hadn't had many opportunities to sit down and talk with
them. We connected mostly over phone and email as needed
and talked about business. Here, we got to talk about *life*, and
life lived fully.

In spending time with Allan, Harry, and Steve, something resonated in a profound way. The conversations we had and the topics we discussed—including music—were things I genuinely cared about and found inspiring. Have ever been around someone or a group of people and had that sense, "these are my people"? That's what I felt while sitting with these guys.

Coming home from that trip, I knew exactly what I needed to do: *become a speaker.*

This wasn't a new idea or desire.

While writing a college paper about "Motivating Your Workforce to Perform" in the mid-1990s, I had fallen in love with the idea of helping people and organizations at intersection of life and work. I just wasn't sure what to do with that idea. Should I become a management consultant? I even considered becoming a pastor at one point. No particular path felt right, and then I landed in the world of booking speakers.

I found fulfillment in putting amazing speakers and their empowering messages in front of audiences. I had the pleasure of booking people like Wayne Dyer, Deepak Chopra, Marcus Buckingham, Naomi Judd, Magic Johnson, Jon Gordon, and others. In working with them, I was happy to play a role in improving lives and businesses.

As the years went by, though, I started sensing that I had something to share, too. I didn't know exactly what, but my hard drive was littered with outlines and drafts of potential talks I could deliver. I was just too scared to do anything with them.

What was new after the trip to San Diego was that I made a *decision* to follow through on what I had been feeling for years.

Desire + Decision = Change.

Without a decision, you just have a wish. A dream.

Anaïs Nin said it beautifully when she wrote, "And the time came when the risk to remain tight in a bud was more painful than the risk it took to blossom."

But what would I speak about? I knew I wanted to inspire people, but "inspiration" is a broad topic. What could *I* share that would be meaningful? What did *I* have credibility to speak about?

I was sitting on the floor of my home office thinking about all of this when a phrase came to me: *this moment matters.*

It hit me that, in facing all the challenges life had thrown my way in recent years, in the midst of all the disappointment and turmoil, there were spaces where I felt a sense of peace: when I just allowed the moment to be what it was. When I didn't fight against the circumstances. In those moments, I was okay.

I also knew that if I wanted to turn my life around, it could only happen one moment at a time. Frankly, whether you are pursuing a big goal or facing a big obstacle, the only way to achieve it or overcome it is one moment at a time.

And, if you want a better relationship, better health, a better business, better sales, better anything, it comes down to the moments.

Life is an accumulation of moments, and all that ever matters is, what will you do with this one?

This moment matters.

That's it. That's my topic.

When I shared this with another one of my good friends, Diane, a fellow speaker, she said, "Have you heard of mindfulness?"

"No," I said.

"You should look into it," she replied. "I think you'd like it."

I did look into it, and I did like it. Turns out, I wasn't the first one to have the idea that "this moment matters." People have been studying it and talking about it for thousands of years. It was new to me, though, and I dove in fully.

Isn't it funny how life works? I was just looking for a speaking topic, but what I found was a phrase, a mantra, and a field that would transform my life.

Within weeks, I had enrolled in that Mindfulness-Based Stress Reduction (MBSR) course at Vanderbilt University in Nashville. Based on the work of a man named Jon Kabat-Zinn, it led me into fields such as Buddhism, psychology, and neuroscience. I was fascinated as my eyes were opened to new realities *and* to see that things I had "felt" for a long time were affirmed by science.

It was in this class and related studies that I learned many of the lessons I shared in the earlier chapters. However, the journey was far from over. I would learn that these tools and practices were useful not only to create my *experience* but to create the *life* I desired. While there were bigger challenges ahead than I could have imagined, each moment, no matter how challenging, was necessary to teach me even deeper lessons about transformation and growth.

Time to Focus

I secured my first paid speaking engagement less than a year after deciding, "I need to become a speaker." It was a breakout session for the Independent Community Bankers of America—a perfect first audience because I had many fond memories at the community bank with my grandma and grandpa. Most involved me going home with a Dum-Dums lollipop.

I still remember people lining up to talk to me after my session, telling me how the message resonated with them. That's always my goal—not to be the "best speaker ever" but to deliver a message that matters to the audience.

One woman, Beverly, the Vice President of a bank in Kansas, said, "Attending this program at the recent convention was one of the most meaningful... being able to truly connect with others and fully enjoy each moment is a gift we've all been given but need to be reminded to embrace in our daily lives."

This early success confirmed I was on the right track, so I looked for more opportunities to speak in person or on a webinar, refining the message as I went. By the end of 2013, I was ready to go all-in.

Having delivered several successful presentations, it was clear the message had value. I saw the escalating problem of people struggling to keep up with the accelerating pace of life and work, so learning how to slow down in the midst of it all brought audiences "a breath of fresh air." As I continued my studies in mindfulness and related fields, my confidence in helping leaders, teams, and organizations grew even stronger.

It was time to reach a broader audience and build a true business that would allow me to do more of this "work I believe in." It was time to take the "this moment matters" message to another level.

To do that, I picked a word for the year ahead: FOCUS. I was determined to make 2014 a pivotal turning point in my journey—and it was... but not in the way I intended or expected.

The Wrong F-Word

For years before, I had allowed myself to become distracted. I would bounce from one direction to another. From one strategy to another. In the end, I felt like I was just spinning in circles. This year would be different, though. I was *focused*.

I was *so* focused and *so* committed to 2014 being different that I enrolled with a coach. This coach had worked successfully with others in my field—speakers, authors, content creators—and he had a plan to achieve the goals I wanted to achieve. He believed so much in his plan that he guaranteed that if I followed this plan for the next 12 months, I would hit my outcomes.

His confidence sparked my confidence, and between his plan and my focus and commitment, I felt unstoppable, like nothing could stand in my way.

But life has a funny way of testing our plans... and our resolve.

For the first few weeks of the new year, everything was going great. I was working overtime in our bonus room, diligently going through the process that was outlined to expand my reach and grow my business. I was making progress, and progress feels good. It's foundational to our happiness.

Almost exactly one month into the year, though, on February 4, everything changed. A medical crisis arose with my wife, although it didn't initially look like a crisis. What we first thought was a *breakthrough* quickly turned into a *breakdown*. And it served as a stark reminder that no plan is immune to the upheavals of life. Guarantees only work in a vacuum.

While my focus *had* been on building the business, now my priorities shifted toward tending to a loved one in need and caring for our young son. That left me only able to work two, three, or four hours a day—which meant I had to ruthlessly focus on the core business, not on new initiatives. And at first, this was fine. It's what you do. Obviously.

After this went on for days, then weeks, and then months, though, I was wearing down and eventually couldn't help but think, "I picked the wrong 'F-word' for this year."

Frustrating is what it was.

What, you were thinking of a different word?

I couldn't believe this was happening again. Another dream dashed. Just when I thought *this time* would be different. But nope. It was like praying for *Knight Rider* all over again. I should explain.

Praying for *Knight Rider*

One morning when I was seven years old, I woke up thinking it was going to be the best day of my life. As a matter of fact, I knew it was going to be the best day of my life. That's because this was the day that *Knight Rider* was coming.

As a boy, *Knight Rider* was my favorite TV show. This was long before the days of streaming TV. If you wanted to watch a show, you had to tune in for it at a set time each week. You had to endure the commercials. There was no premium plan that would allow you to opt out.

And every week, we *did* tune in to watch *Knight Rider*. I was captivated from the moment the theme song began. Then, the narrator spoke:

"A shadowy flight into the dangerous world of a man who does not exist. Michael Knight, a young loner on a crusade, to champion the cause of the innocent, the helpless, the powerless. In a world of criminals who operate above the law..."

Michael Knight in his black leather jacket was my hero.

Although, I have to say, no offense to David Hasselhoff, it was really all about the car. Mostly about the car, anyway—his car tech, Bonnie, was pretty cute, too.

But that car. If you know, you know.

Knight Industries Two Thousand, or KITT, if you prefer.

Sleek, shiny, black. As many lights and buttons as a jumbo jet cockpit, it seemed. Not to mention, it could drive itself. It could talk to you. I recently rented a Hyundai that had many of the same features, but back in 1984, this was amazing. And on this morning, I was going to see KITT in person, in my driveway.

Making this even more remarkable is the fact that I grew up three miles down a red dirt road in rural Missouri. More than two thousand miles from where the show filmed in Burbank, California. I wasn't worried about that, though.

I had no doubt *Knight Rider* was coming on this day because... I had prayed for *Knight Rider* to come. And between lessons from Sunday School and watching Oral Roberts with my grandma, I heard that "if you ask and you believe, then you shall receive."

Seriously?! You can ask for anything?!! Those are powerful words.

To my knowledge, there was no fine print on this "ask, believe, and receive" thing, so... at seven years old, seeing *Knight Rider* as the greatest thing on earth, I thought, if I can ask for anything, and if I just believe it, then it will happen... then give me a visit from *Knight Rider*.

So, that was my prayer on the preceding Friday night, and when Saturday morning came, all I had to do was wait for it. I was so excited!

I went out into our front yard that morning and I looked to the left, through the trees and brush, to where the road magically appeared and made a sharp turn into a straight stretch in front of our house. My eyes were fixated on that curve. That's where I knew I would get the first glimpse of that black shiny car and that red light flashing across the front. That's where magic was going to happen.

It didn't happen in the first few minutes I was watching, though.

It didn't happen in the first few hours.

No matter. I paced back in forth in the front yard. I played in the sandbox. I went inside to eat, peeking out the window periodically. Then back outside to pace some more.

I didn't tell my parents how special this day was going to be. No one knew but me, so I waited and waited. The anticipation was almost unbearable.

I could see it all happening in my mind. KITT coming down our long gravel driveway. Pulling off into the grass. The doors opening. Me getting to look inside. Getting to sit inside, even, in those camel tan cloth seats.

At some point in the day, though, the anticipation turned to doubt. The doubt turned to sadness. As the sun began to set on that day, I came to realize what you already know... which is that *Knight Rider* isn't coming.

When I share this story with audiences, this is where a collective "aww" often comes across the room. It is a sad story, and I appreciate the sympathy, but I also know the reason the story "hits" is because it's one that we can all relate to. Who hasn't had a childhood dream dashed somewhere along the way? This experience has obviously stuck with me for years.

Of course, when you're a child, having your dreams dashed is disappointing. As you get older, though, the stakes get higher. It's not a fictional TV character that doesn't show up, but it's the healing of a loved one that doesn't come. It's the relationship miracle that doesn't come. It's the financial breakthrough that doesn't come. It's the career or business turnaround that doesn't come.

It's not only disappointing. It's discouraging. Demoralizing. Depressing.

So many times, I had felt like I was just hitting my stride, and then, bam.

In all these endings, I couldn't see a new beginning.

As a matter of fact, at one point, I described the experience as feeling like I was living in a prison cell. Trapped. No way out. I could close my eyes and dream of the life I wanted, but then I would wake up and find myself right back in my cell again. Miserable. Empty. I hated it.

Now, despite my best efforts, I was right back here again in 2014.

Even with all the tools I had for *Mastering the Moments*, I didn't know what to do next. So, I did something I was very uncomfortable doing: I asked for help.

You're Not Wrong...

While I had been pretty good at picking myself up in the past, I was struggling to "see the light" when my guaranteed plan of 2014 was upended. I was confused and just needed somebody to speak into this situation. That's when I reached out to a local pastor named Blake and asked for a meeting.

Blake obliged, and I drove to his office in downtown Nashville. I nervously sat down across from him, not sure what I would say, and not sure what he would say. But it felt like I was in the right place.

He asked how I was doing, and I filled him in on how the year had unfolded. I summed it up by saying, "It's been pretty tough," somewhat dismissive of it all.

Blake wasn't fooled.

"I'd say that's the understatement of the century," he replied.

It was clear this was going to be a no-bullshit session. I was just looking for some comfort and encouragement, but Blake wasn't into that so much.

"I look at you and I see someone who's bleak, oppressed, hopeless," he said as the conversation continued. Talk about comfort and encouragement. I definitely called the right guy.

In all seriousness, though, he was spot-on. His assessment was a mirror reflecting the harsh reality of my condition.

It felt like I had hit a wall. But how had I arrived here again, now equipped with tools to transform any moment, yet feeling utterly defeated and powerless?

I thought I had found the secret to being content in all things. But were these tools not as powerful as I had thought? Was I a fraud in sharing this message?

The truth is, I was not in the same place I was in back in 2008. Then, I said I was lost, empty, and depressed. Not only were the words different this time, but the pain was different. The suffering was different.

To struggle to find or embrace your purpose, as I had for many years, will leave you feeling lost, empty, and depressed. To feel that you *know* your purpose and yet feel that you're blocked from *living* it is absolutely tormenting. That's what leaves you feeling bleak, oppressed, and hopeless.

While it's true, I had developed the ability to be content in all things, there were things in my life that I was tolerating—or, really, ignoring—which needed my attention.

If you look at your life, I wonder if you see the same. Are there parts of your life where you feel good, happy, fulfilled—or at least like you kind of know what you're doing? And then are there other areas where you feel like, "Man, if they only knew..."?

On the outside, it looked like I had it "all together," but really, I was still living in survival mode—just a more elegant form of it than before. And it had become a comfortable place to be. *I can find contentment without stepping outside my comfort zone.* That's wonderful. Until it isn't.

Working intently to build my career—something I truly cared about—had given me an escape from attending to a critical area of my life, my marriage, which had become profoundly unhealthy over nearly a decade. I knew what to do in business—whether I executed it perfectly or not. I was at a loss for what to do in my marriage. So, I just let it be. I was just trying to get through it.

As we learned from Brody, anytime you find yourself trying to get through something, you're in survival mode. And while survival mode is okay for a season, it's not okay for a lifetime.

Just like when I was changing Brody's diaper years ago, I was once again feeling the pull toward something more. I believe that's what crisis does for us.

While I felt like I had hit a wall, what I've found is that if you zoom out, it's not a wall. It's a step, inviting you, calling you, urging you, to rise to another level.

Or, said another way, what looks like "the end" is an opportunity for a new beginning. And before I would leave my new mentor Blake's office, I would be able to see it more clearly than ever before.

He asked me some more questions, some tough questions, which led to me saying some things that I would have never imagined telling anyone. Nothing surprised him, though.

How could you know I would be thinking these thoughts? I wondered.

Then, he said the three words that I didn't know I needed to hear, but which changed my life: "You're not wrong…"

"You're not wrong to want a better life for yourself and your son," he told me.

Whoa. I was not expecting to hear those words on this day. And definitely not from a pastor.

"Would you feel guilty if you left?" he asked. "Maybe. Probably. But would that guilt be from God?"

I shook my head.

"No, it wouldn't," he said.

I don't remember any of the conversation after that. What I do know, though, is that I went into that meeting feeling beaten down, looking for nothing but encouragement, but I walked out feeling an energetic charge that I hadn't felt in years. What I was feeling was a sense of *freedom*.

He gave me the permission that I didn't know I needed, to listen to myself.

The reality is, I didn't just want a better life for me and my son. I wanted a better life for my wife, too. But it had become clear to me that this better life wasn't possible as long as our marriage stayed intact.

The truth is, I had been wrestling with our marriage for years. Deep down, I knew that "this isn't right"—speaking of our marriage dynamics—but I also had a belief that "divorce is wrong." I had a belief that "I can't divorce." I even wrote those words in my journal.

This is where I could plant the seeds for a spinoff book about religious baggage. Instead, I'll just say this: Your beliefs will either propel you to new heights or block you from living the life you're called to live. In this case, my beliefs were holding all of us back. They kept me locked in a relationship for well over a decade after it had become profoundly unhealthy.

What began as love, patience, compassion, and accommodation had sunk into all-out codependency. I was as much a part of the unhealthy dynamic as she was. In trying to accommodate her needs, I enabled behaviors that were not healthy for either of us. I thought that was my role. I thought that was love. But love should elevate, not enable.

I had "allowed" all of this over the years while continuing to make efforts to move forward in my business. The reality, though, is that I had become complacent and accepted "survival mode" in my marriage. I was truly just trying to get through it.

I came to see that what I thought was compassion, what I thought was accommodation, was cruelly enabling her debilitating behaviors. I was not helping her. I was only digging the hole deeper and deeper for both of us. Still, those beliefs about divorce kept me stuck.

For years I had wanted a better life, but I was certain that desire was wrong. More than that, I was certain *I* was wrong to have it. That's what a belief is: a thought you hold with certainty. And until that day in Blake's office, every counselor I had spoken to had reinforced that belief.

One marriage counselor we saw suggested we simply "stay present." This was hilarious considering I had dedicated my life and work to staying present at that point. *I know how to stay present*, I thought. And then I asked him, "Would you say the same to someone in an abusive situation, or someone living with an alcoholic?"

That wasn't my story, but there were parallels and this registered to me as horrible counsel. Staying present, I suppose that at every moment other than the moment when you're being abused, you would say, "Well, she's not hitting me right now." And then you continue for another day?

Another renowned therapist and best-selling author I spoke to suggested I go on antidepressants just to endure it. I'm all for medication when needed. But I thought, *you want me to take medication to simply numb the pain and numb the feeling that this isn't right? What?!*

Somewhere along the way, a dear friend pointed out something that I had never considered. A marriage counselor's aim is to save the marriage, not the person. I'm sure there are exceptions to that, but that aligned perfectly with my experience.

These therapists were telling me, in effect, I *was* wrong to want a better life. Even though the one who told me to take antidepressants also told me that he had seen cases like mine, and the only time he had seen the woman get better was after divorce. Interesting.

While I disagreed with these therapists, I shared their belief that divorce was wrong. As a matter of fact, I had said the same thing to my younger brother when his marriage was crumbling years before. Looking back, that's some of the worst advice I've ever given.

Note to self: don't tell someone what's right or wrong if you haven't walked in their shoes.

These counselors were trying to help me, just as I was trying to help my brother, but ultimately, *you* are the one who knows what you truly need to do. And the sooner you can come to trust yourself, the sooner you can step into a more aligned, more authentic life.

Even after hearing, "you're not wrong to want a better life," I still tried and tried and tried to make the marriage work. Breaking free from the beliefs that have shaped your identity is hard to do. And so is breaking free from the bonds of codependency.

The last thing I wanted to do was hurt this woman, a friend, I cared about. Learning that hurt and harm are not synonymous was another key point on this journey. Some decisions that hurt initially pave the way for healing and growth, long-term.

Somewhere in the unfolding of 2014, I read Mary Oliver's amazing poem, *The Journey*, for the first time. I had known *of* it, but I had never read it. When I did, I knew it was a divine encounter.

From the first words—"One day you finally knew what you had to do, and began"—to the last—"determined to save the only life you could save"—she was speaking to me.

It's important to have others tell you you're not wrong to want a better life. At some point, though, you must know it for yourself. Only then can you truly move forward. For someone who is a natural-born caregiver, it's hard to learn—and then embrace—that the only life they can truly save is their own.

Boundaries are something I learned about far too late in life, and I'm still catching up. Boundaries aren't just necessary for your own wellbeing, but for those you care about, too. Prentis Hemphill writes so beautifully, "Boundaries are the distance at which I can love you and me simultaneously."

Indeed, sometimes loving means leaving.

What I believe now is that God is not so concerned with saving a manmade relationship that they are willing to sacrifice either of the individuals involved. God loves *you*, the person, and *your partner*, but what kind of God would love a marriage that perpetuates a cycle of pain and limitation for the people involved?

Don't read that to mean that I don't value marriage. I believe that a union of two humans coming together to support one another and strengthen one another and be a beacon of light and love to those around them is one of the most amazing things. That is something to be celebrated and honored and protected.

Likewise, don't think I am an advocate of divorce.

I'm all for pushing through pain and difficulty. That's a big part of what *Mastering the Moments* is about. However, in relationships, pushing through pain and difficulty only works when both parties take responsibility for themselves. I would never advise a couple to save the relationship at the expense of the individual.

This isn't a license to be selfish, but rather a command to honor the dignity of each person. When you have two healthy individuals who hold that space for one another, you create something beautiful.

From Focus to Flexibility

At the start of 2014, my focus was on my business. By the end, my focus had shifted to something far more personal, which I could no longer ignore: my marriage. It was the one thing that could change everything.

In the process, I realized that I had indeed picked the wrong "F-word" at the start of the year. *Flexibility* was the real key. You must be clear on where you're going—in this case, in pursuit of a life of authenticity and alignment—but flexible in how you get there.

By the end of the year, while I hadn't turned my business around, I was preparing to move—with my son—out of the house where I had lived for almost 10 years. I signed the lease on a two-bedroom apartment across town. It would be a better school district for him to start kindergarten, our neighbors had just moved in that direction, and the church we attended at the time was opening a new campus there.

Once again, an overwhelming number of "moments" indicated that this was the right move, and I could see the new beginning up ahead. But it was, without a doubt, still a painful ending. That move across town required far more courage than when I moved hundreds of miles across the country to Nashville at 17. That's because I had to break free from some of those old beliefs in order to do it.

Moving to Nashville was big, but I was doing something you're "supposed" to do—go to college, follow your dreams. Moving across town 20 years later, though, I was doing something you're *not* "supposed" to do—separating from your spouse (so I believed).

It was a move I had known—deep down—that I needed to make for years, but I thought my marriage was untouchable. *I can't divorce.* What is that? It's just a belief. *Can* you? Yes. The legal system allows for it. Do you *want* to do it? That's up to you. You can seek out counsel to help you work through that decision. But *can* you? Yes, absolutely. You can. But it takes tremendous courage to be true to yourself.

When you break free from old beliefs, it's also breaking free from an old identity. And there's nothing we cling to more tightly than our identity. A big part of my identity was, "I'm someone who doesn't get divorced. I'm someone who stays with my partner through anything."

If you want a better life, though, it's going to start with up-grading your identity. Everything starts on the inside.

By the end of 2014, I did not achieve the guaranteed results in my business. No wonder, because I wasn't able to follow the plan. So that nullified the guarantee. But by the end of the year, what I did achieve was something even more meaningful.

Trials and challenges, I've come to believe, do not show up as obstacles to you achieving your goals. They come up to force you to examine your goals—and values, and purpose—more deeply. Life gives you exactly what you need to rise up and move forward.

If you have a vision for a change that is better for you and ultimately for others, as well, you're not wrong. As a matter of fact, if that change has been calling out to you for a while, your desire just might be divine.

Your Desire Is Divine

In preparing to write this book, I came across a letter I wrote to God in 2006. That was when I was still looking for God to save me. Waiting for *Knight Rider* to come, in effect.

"I need help," I wrote.

Seeking help, I went to the Bible, which was all I knew to do at that time. This was back in the days of writing my "Peace in the Storm" blog and newsletter.

"I'm looking back at Genesis. Sometimes the answers are in the beginning."

Indeed, the answers were—and are—right there, but I missed them.

I captured the first verse of Genesis, the first book in the Bible, in my letter:

> "In the beginning, God cre-
> ated the heavens and the
> earth." (Genesis 1:1, NIV)

At that time, my takeaway was that since God is the same yesterday, today, and forever, then God can speak things into existence today just the same as in the beginning.

"He rules the world with intelligence and mastery like I know how to make a PB&J sandwich," I wrote.

(While my language has evolved since then, reflecting a more inclusive view of God, I'm quoting my journal as written to remain true to my mindset and writing at that time.)

After looking at some additional verses and capturing my commentary, I wrote, "What do I do? Please 'speak' into my life. Just as you did in the beginning. Make something out of nothing. Create order out of chaos."

That was all I knew to do. And it kept me stuck.

Reading it all these years later, though, I see that the answers were right in front of me. They *are* in the beginning!

You see, in 2006, I was reading the Bible to understand the nature of God and to increase my belief or trust that God could resolve my situation—particularly related to my marriage. *I* can't do anything, but God can. That was my belief. And that's how I lived many years of my life. To the point that on my best days, I would pray for God to change my circumstances, and on my worst days, I would pray for my life to end. Either way, I was powerless.

There's another verse in the Bible that says, "God is love." (1 John 4:8)

Would love want its own creation to be powerless?

If that's too abstract, would you want your own child—or someone you care deeply about—to be powerless?

Of course not. And neither did—does—God.

I *wasn't* powerless.

I'm *not* powerless.

And neither are you.

Go back to the beginning.

We are told that "in the beginning, God created..."

What does that make God, then?

It's not a trick question.

Someone who creates is a... *creator.*

Right. God is a creator.

Now let's skip ahead to the 26th verse:

> "Let us make human beings
> in our image, make them re-
> flecting our nature..."
> (Genesis 1:26, The Message)

In other words, as God is, *we* are, *you* are, *I* am.

If God is a creator, and you and I are created in God's image, then we are... *creators.*

And what do creators do?

They create!

Not only are you the creator of your experience, as we've established, but you are the creator of your life. As the creator, you are absolutely not wrong to want a better life! If that's what you want to create—as long as it is not harmful to yourself or others—then you have the license to create it.

This is what I was missing all those years ago. I was reading the Bible to understand the nature of God, but I failed to see what it was saying about the nature of *me*—and *you*.

Now, let's shift from spiritual talk to science for a moment.

While taking a course on "Finding Purpose and Meaning in Life" with Vic Stretcher at the University of Michigan—it's free, you can take it, too!—I learned something fascinating.

When you think about your purpose or what you value in life, a part of your brain called the ventromedial prefrontal cortex (vmPFC) lights up. The vmPFC is heavily involved in processes related to self-reflection, decision-making, and evaluating the significance of different experiences and goals. So, when you're contemplating your purpose or pondering your values, this brain region is where a lot of the action is.

Now, here's the fascinating part: The vmPFC is located just behind the forehead, in the area that some traditions identify as the third eye or your highest self. What if modern science is now supporting what ancient spiritual traditions have always known—that when you contemplate your purpose in life, or your values, or your direction, you are tapping into the highest part of yourself?

Whether you look at it through a spiritual lens or a scientific one, my view is that your desire—that idea or drive that won't let you go—is divine. As divine as Jesus—who exemplified the divine in human form—saying to his early disciples, "Come, follow me."

Joseph Murphy writes, "Desire is an angel of God, telling us something which, if accepted by us, will make our life fuller and happier."

No wonder, then, that if you continue to ignore, deny, or suppress this divine desire, you will find yourself feeling bleak, oppressed, or hopeless. You are truly holding back the divine within you. When you choose to embrace it, though, you'll find the path toward a life filled with peace, joy, excitement, and passion.

That's why I say, when you have one of those desires that won't let you go—or that you can't let go of—"you should do that!" The more you learn to say "yes" to these yearnings—these divine desires—the richer your life will become.

Does that mean it won't be scary? No, it most certainly will be.

Does that mean it will all go smoothly? No, it most certainly will not.

But is there anything better than knowing you're living the life you're called to? Absolutely not.

Chapter 4

What Is the Right Thing, Right Now?

The Safe Route Isn't the Safe Route

ONCE YOU FINALLY EMBRACE your identity as the creator of your life, when you recognize that you're not wrong to want a better life, and more than that, your desire is divine, then it's time to act.

I previously shared my story of moving into an apartment with my son, and how that move took more courage than moving to Nashville when I was 17. Anytime you get clear on where you want to go, you can be sure that stepping into that clarity is going to require you to step outside of your comfort zone. The thing is, we don't like to step outside of our comfort zone.

As humans, we're wired with something known as expediency bias, which means if there is a familiar path, that's the way we're going to go. That's not a bad thing. It's part of our survival mechanism. Your brain wants to keep you safe, and stepping outside of your comfort zone, doing something that's unfamiliar or uncertain, registers as danger. Danger registers as a chance of death.

I heard something from Elizabeth Gilbert, author of books like *Eat Pray Love* and *Big Magic*, in the years leading up to my divorce that hit me hard: "The safe route is not the safe route."

It hit me because I had taken the safe route for much of my life. I was a rule follower. (Still am in many ways.) I did what you're supposed to do. Went to bed early. Studied. Got good grades. Ate a balanced diet. Married my best friend. Put in the extra effort.

From a young age, while I always had my dad in my ear saying, "You can do anything! You can be anything you want to be!" I also had my parents in my ear saying, "Be careful."

As a young boy, there was an elm tree at my grandparents' house that I loved to climb. It was awesome. There was a fork low enough that I could step up into it. From there, I could grab the next limb and hoist myself up. *I bet I could climb to the top*, I thought. I never did, though.

"Don't go any higher," I would hear. "You might fall and break your arm."

So, I climbed back down.

It's tough to achieve your dreams and be all you want to be if you live in constant fear of getting hurt. My parents would tell you today—as they've told me—that they were too protective of me as a child.

I don't blame them. They were doing what they thought was best.

I'm the one who chose to hold on to the "be careful" advice for longer than was necessary. That's a big reason why I lived years of my life feeling like I was stuck in a loop. It felt like I was watching repeats of the same episodes over and over again. *How did I end up here again?*

My work has been to learn to honor this voice inside that says, "be careful," and know that it's only trying to keep me safe. Not only that, but to keep me alive. While I honor it, I have also had to learn to, at times, remind it that, "I'm okay, I understand the risk here."

Most of the time, the risks required to follow our dreams and desires—to do that thing we know we're supposed to do—don't put our lives at risk. There's usually not a sabretooth tiger hiding behind the bush, although our reptilian brain responds to risk as if there could be.

To not follow those dreams and desires, while technically "safe," can feel like death for our soul. Your mind understands nothing about the soul and what makes it feel alive.

After years of taking the safe route, my physical body was safe, but I felt dead inside. As I started pushing myself to step into discomfort, though, what I found is that the *idea* of the new thing is always scarier than the new thing itself.

Here We Go

When my friend Justin and I went skydiving a few years ago, we had the choice of jumping from 11,000 feet, 15,000 feet, or 18,000 feet. Eighteen thousand feet is the highest altitude you can jump from as a civilian skydiver.

My thought was, we definitely don't want to do 11,000 feet. I mean, come on! There's less time to freefall, and it would be over too fast. I figured 15,000 feet would be just fine, though. No need to get too crazy. Just that "middle of the road" experience. There's that "safe route" mentality showing up—even while doing something that some would say is unsafe.

Justin is the opposite of me in many ways, though. He lives for adventure. He takes chances. He is bold. And he has had some amazing experiences as a result. His view was, "We're probably only going to do this once in our lifetime, so let's go all the way!"

I couldn't argue with that, so we signed up for the 18,000-foot jump. I remember when we were going through the orientation process, one of the guys said, "This is your first time? And you're going to 18,000 feet?"

"Yep," we replied. That's what happens when you surround yourself with friends who push you to go higher. In this case, literally.

We climbed into the plane—us and four other jumpers, with their tandem partners and a couple of videographers. The plane spiraled up to the target altitude. I'm looking out the window, taking in the scene. I love flying.

At one point, I saw a fragment of a rainbow in a cloud. I pointed it out to my tandem partner with excitement. "And look, there's a unicorn, too!" he replied. Smartass.

Finally, we reached 11,000 feet. Time for the first ~~victims~~ jumpers to make their exit. I watched as they scooted toward the open door at the back of the plane. The first jumper with her tandem partner got into position, sitting on the very edge. Before I knew it, they had disappeared. Poof!

Another jumper at this altitude, and then we spiraled up toward 15,000 feet. Again, I watched as the next jumpers went through the same process, scooting toward the door, sitting right on the edge. Poof! They were gone.

Now it was just Justin and me—and our tandem partners—left in the plane. Well, and the pilot. And our videographers. To 18,000 feet we go.

Justin went first. My stomach churns a bit as I replay this in my mind. Soon, he was gone. My turn. *Holy shit.*

My tandem partner and I scooted toward the edge. I'm in front of him (of course). He told me to hook my legs back under the plane. He said he was going to count down, and then we were going to jump, and we'd do a backflip, and... I'm not sure what he said after that.

Next thing I knew, we were out of the plane, caught in what felt like a blanket of air. The video shows that we did a backflip. I don't remember it, though.

I had dreams as a kid about falling off my grandparents' roof—two stories up—and I would always have that sensation in my stomach like when you make that first drop on a roller coaster. You know, where your stomach ends up in your throat?

I wondered if that would be my experience in skydiving, but it was nothing like that. What I remember is feeling like I was caught in a blanket of air. Of course, I wasn't caught. We were falling at a rate of over 100 miles an hour. But the speed and air pressure felt like being caught.

I felt safe.

When you do scary things, it often feels like that.

All the fear and worry and doubt and anxiety come *before* you do the thing. You contemplate and magnify everything that could go wrong. If other people are involved, you "know" exactly how they will react—and it's never good. You are your own worst boogeyman.

Then when you do *do* the thing, even if it's uncomfortable, you realize you're fine. You have the feeling of safety. Like, *ah, yes! I'm doing it!*

When Brody and I first went to visit our new apartment, as scary as that move was, it also had a feeling of joy about it. A feeling of a new beginning. A feeling of hope. A feeling of excitement.

I still remember, we picked up food from Zaxby's (a chicken tender restaurant) on the way and I sat him on top of the kitchen island to eat. That memory brings tears to my eyes.

I'm not going to lie and tell you there's *no* discomfort with doing the scary things. While my stomach didn't feel like it was in my throat after jumping out of the plane, I did find it hard to breathe. And the air pressure was killing my ears!

They told us, "If you struggle to breathe, yell."

I yelled. And I still struggled to breathe. And I had impaired hearing out of one of my ears for about two months after the experience. But I also thought to myself, *You know what, if this hearing loss is permanent, I'll take it in exchange for having had that experience.*

The safe route isn't the safe route, and the "dangerous" route usually isn't truly dangerous, either.

Let me add a note here: I am not advising you to make stupid, crazy, careless, reckless moves in your life. Use your brain. Talk to friends, mentors, therapists, or coaches. Just don't allow fear to keep you stuck.

The magic happens when you step into your divine desires. The key word there is *step*.

Just Say Yes

To follow your dreams doesn't require that you take a giant leap all the time. It doesn't mean you have to pick up and move across town. It doesn't mean you have to jump out of an airplane. Sometimes courage looks like that, but if you look closely, you'll see that often times even the biggest jumps start with a small step. So small that if you weren't looking for it, you wouldn't even notice.

At my speaking events, I will sometimes demonstrate this by asking the audience to stand up (all who are able). Then I direct them to step out where they've got a little bit of space in front of them. I ask them to take their best power pose—whether that's hands on their hips, or with a fist in the sky, whatever it is. Then I ask them to do something really crazy:

Take one step forward.

That's it.

Sometimes, courage looks like that.

And, as silly as it may seem, it's actually a great picture of courage. Audience members don't know what they're about to do when I ask them to stand up. Surely there are some nerves that come with that. *Am I going to have to talk to people?* (That's my first thought when I'm a participant, anyway. I'll do anything. Just please don't make me talk to people.)

But they just take it one step at a time. Stand up. Make a power pose. Take a step forward.

Oh, that's it? We're done? That wasn't so bad.

Exactly.

Even if you take something that looks big—and is big—like moving to Nashville, skydiving, starting a business, getting married, getting a divorce, getting on stage to speak, it actually starts quite small.

Before I moved into that apartment with Brody, I wrote in my journal for months, taking note of my reality, observing the situation, talking with others, processing my thoughts, reading words of wisdom, envisioning my future if I didn't make a change, envisioning a new future *if* I made a change. Then once I had made a decision, I started looking at apartments, calculating costs, making a plan. Then once I found a possible apartment, I had to make a call. Send an email. Go visit.

That big move was actually just the next right step in the process.

What is the right thing, right now?

This is a journey of *Mastering the Moments*, remember?

Knowing that life is an accumulation of moments, the question is always, what will you do with *this one*?

Take me speaking on stage.

Before I had ever gone to see Sawyer Brown or had a conscious desire to pursue a career in music, it seemed that I was destined to be on stage. My MaMa used to love to tell the story of me being four or five years old at a family reunion, standing on a table with my little guitar and cowboy hat singing along to Billy "Crash" Craddock's song, "Rub It In." The funny thing, she remembered, though, was that I couldn't say my r's, so my version was, "Wub it in, wub it in."

There was the "performance" aspect of speaking showing up. Then with my other grandma, I was so interested in watching Oral Roberts with her—and sending him my nickels and dimes—that she called me her "little preacher man." There was the "inspirational" piece of speaking.

Beyond that, there was something in me that was just always drawn to coming alongside people in times of difficulty. Whether it was lying on the floor next to my seven-year-old brother when he was in a full-leg cast or walking across town after junior high to sit with my grandfather in his hospital room after surgery or going to play piano and sing to nursing home residents, it was just "in me."

With all that, you'd think that it was just a natural progression for me to end up as a speaker now. *Of course that's what you're doing now.*

But nope, that's not how it went.

When I first started sharing pictures or videos of me speaking on social media, some of my friends from elementary school and high school were shocked. *What?! You're a speaker now?!* That's because they knew me to be one of the shyest kids in school. Because I was.

I was so painfully shy that I would poop my pants at school—because "going number two" in public was too uncomfortable. Not only that, but I remember one day in third grade, Miss Weiker's class, when I needed to go number one. I raised my hand and waited, hoping, praying for her to call on me. Problem was, she wasn't even looking at me. She was writing on the chalkboard. (This was before the days of whiteboards, kids.)

Even when she turned around to talk to the class, she wasn't noticing me. I was waving my hand and squirming, doing my best to hold it in. All I had to do was say, "Miss Weiker," and she would have let me go. But I was too shy to speak up.

Finally, when she did call on me—"Shawn?"—all I could say was, "It's too late."

The puddle forming under my chair gave me away.

I learned two things that day. First, always go to the bathroom before class. Second, embarrassment won't kill you. It just feels like it might. But that was how shy I was as a kid. So, the idea of public speaking as a career path was not one that ever crossed my mind.

Actually, when I was in college, "speech" was one of our required courses. I hated that class. It was my lowest grade throughout my college career. I got a C.

How did that shy kid end up as a successful speaker?

One step at a time.

Day by day, I built up my courage muscle.

I pressed through the fear to show up for band auditions—with aspiring artists, the Opryland theme park, and even Lee Greenwood. You know, Mr. "God Bless the USA"?

One day, while in college, I came home to find a message from him on my answering machine. He said, "Hey Shawn, this is Lee Greenwood. I got your name and number. I'm moving this week, but I'd love for you to come over to the house and audition for me."

Wow! Me?! Absolutely.

I remember going to his house in Nashville. The movers are actually there. The house is emptying out. But there in the entryway is this beautiful white grand piano. So, I go in and he said, "Play me some moving music."

I love to play moving music. You know, that easy listening, New Age style piano like Jim Brickman or Yanni. That is my jam. It's so *moving*.

That clearly wasn't what he was looking for. He meant music that *moves*. Music that would make the *movers* want to move. I love playing that, too. Give me some good, dirty, New Orleans jazz style piano. Oh yeah. But that's not what I played that day. And so, I didn't get the gig.

But I auditioned for Lee Greenwood. And I didn't die.

Once again, it was scary going into it, but afterward, "Cool! I did that. And I survived."

Nearly a decade later, after I had left my "professional" music dreams behind, I was working on staff at a church and playing piano for the choir and worship team. It was a small church, and there came a time when the two pastors were going to be out of town for an event. They needed someone to speak and I said, "I'll do it."

"Really?" they asked.

I'm sure they were thinking the same thing my friends thought. *You? The guy who never talks?*

The day came and I remember sitting up on stage as the announcements were being read, waiting until it was my turn to speak. When the person introduced me, I remember feeling like there was a force field holding me in my chair. I couldn't move. But somehow, I broke free and started walking toward the pulpit. It was like busting through a brick wall at that point. I made some joke about Bon Jovi—probably the first of many clues that the pulpit was not the place I was destined to speak—and we were off.

I had a blast. I spoke about "living by the Spirit," and I remember a little girl in the audience gave me a piece of paper afterward—a picture she had drawn of me speaking, that just had a speech bubble that said, "Holy Spirit." I guess my point was clear!

That feeling of being scared, feeling stuck, and then breaking through, has never left me, though. I think about it every time I speak. When I get nervous, I remember that the feeling will pass, I will step into it, and we'll have a good time. We always do.

Not long after the church event, I saw an ad looking for people to speak to high school students. It was a program sponsored by Monster.com and they had a program called "Making College and Career Count." They needed speakers to deliver a 45-minute scripted presentation.

I sent in my little audition video, got invited to their weekend workshop, got selected as one of their speakers. I memorized the talk and then proceeded to do a series of events for high school students in the region. My largest audience was around a thousand students at a private school in Nashville.

What I learned in that experience is that students are a tough audience!

I always got top marks from the teachers and adults in the room, and "decent" marks from the students. I quickly realized that adults are my audience. I have friends who specialize in student programs and I have tremendous respect for them. It is its own kind of talent.

This was all years before standing over Brody's changing table, but my courage muscle was being strengthened with every new experience. When I did finally decide to put myself "out there" with my own message, it was still one step at a time:

Buy a domain name.

Enroll in Mindfulness-Based Stress Reduction course.

Attend industry association conference.

Pitch myself as a speaker.

I just kept saying "yes" when life served up opportunities.

Now, more than a decade after hanging up my official "speaker" flag with the "this moment matters" message, I never know where or when the next opportunity will be... but I'm grateful for every one.

And when someone comes up to me after an event, or after hearing that I speak, and says, "Wow, I could never do that!" I always think, "Oh yes you can." If I can, you can.

There's a distinction we need to make when talking about taking things "one step at a time." Telling you about the steps I took toward moving out with Brody, or the steps I took toward building my speaking business, it starts to sound like it was all very linear. It's not.

When I look back over my journey, I took several steps that weren't the best steps. They were simply the right thing to do at that time. That's the question, remember:

What is the right thing, right now?

That's all you can ever do.

The only wrong thing is to sit on the sidelines analyzing all the possible paths, only to then do... nothing.

So, think about your own journey. Is there a move you've been wanting to make for a long time, but fear has been holding you back? Maybe you can't take the giant leap today, but you don't have to. What is the biggest step—no matter how small—you can take today toward a vision or a dream?

Remember, it's not about making monumental leaps every day. Sometimes, it's about standing up, taking a deep breath, and moving one foot forward.

If you find yourself on the edge, hesitating because of fear or doubt, remember: you're not wrong to want a better life. Every big change starts with a decision to try. So take that step. Embrace the possibility of discomfort as the path to growth. You've done it before, and you can do it again.

If you want to experience something you've never experienced, you're going to have to do something that you've never done. And if you ask me, you should do that.

Mastering the Moments is about learning to "say yes" to your divine desires, and then leave what happens next up to Life. What I've found is that when you take actions that are aligned with your vision, the Universe supports you in mysterious ways.

Chapter 5

Be That Which You Seek

What Do You Really Want?

YOUR VISION FOR YOUR life surely has some tangible targets—like I wanted a visit from *Knight Rider*, a better marriage, and to become a speaker. But what do you *really* want?

We often fail to make the distinction between vehicles and values. For example, maybe you *value* financial freedom, and a six-figure job is the *vehicle* that you think will bring it.

So often, we place our focus on the outer circumstances that we want to change or experience in our lives, without realizing that it's not really the circumstances we want, but what we think they will bring us. What we value, though, can often be found in this very moment. But it's hard to find it if you don't know what it is, so let me introduce you to an exercise that I learned during the worst therapy appointment ever.

When my first post-divorce relationship ended, it rocked my world. Now, here I was divorced, still struggling financially, and also wondering if I would ever find the ideal partner. Once again, I realized I needed help, and this time, I was looking for a therapist.

Thankfully, the church I was attending had a relationship with an area college so you could see one of their interns for a limited number of sessions at no charge. That fit perfectly with my budget, so I made an appointment.

I showed up to this little brick outbuilding where the counseling interns saw patients. I signed in at the window and sat down in the tiny waiting room to... wait. Ah, the liminal space again.

When the door finally opened and the young man said, "Shawn?" I was ready. But I was not ready for what I experienced.

It was clear early on that he was a nervous mess. He was medium height, a bit of a stocky build, with a scruffy beard. Altogether, I couldn't tell if he was 24 or 37.

He walked me back to the non-descript office—very bland and clinical feeling, with tile floors, basic office chairs, and no identifying decorations.

As he began reading through the disclaimers from the sheet on his clipboard, he was very tentative, and his voice sounded shaky. I was already beginning to doubt the value of this session. Of course, you know what I paid, so... I guess the value was already established.

After getting through the formalities, he began working through the background questions on his clipboard. When he asked, "So, what's been going on?" my first thought was, *You're not ready for this.* But also, I thought, *you're here to learn, so I'm gonna give you all of it and we'll see what happens.*

I walked him through all the challenges in my life. The financial struggles. The relationship woes. The parenting headaches.

Remember when I met with Blake and told him about everything, and he said, "I look at you and I see someone who's bleak, oppressed, hopeless"? Remember when he told me that me saying it had been "pretty tough" was the "understatement of the century"? Remember when he told me, "You're not wrong to want a better life"? Clearly, there would be no such wisdom on this day.

After sharing everything that was weighing on me, his response was a monotone, "That sounds tough." I wanted to say, "Okay, let's try that once more, but this time with feeling!"

After getting through the elementary questions, he said to me, "Imagine you went to sleep tonight and overnight, while you slept, there was a miracle. When you wake up in the morning, everything in your life is exactly as you would want it to be. What would you need to see to know that there had been a miracle?"

I thought to myself, *Okay, so we're playing make believe now. Wonderful.*

But I played along.

I said, "Well, I would be in a healthy, loving relationship. My son would be thriving—doing well in school, happy, healthy. I would be doing work I love. I would be debt-free and my bank account would be overflowing with a surplus of funds."

"Okay, good," he said. "And how would you feel seeing all that?"

After some thought, I said, "Happy, I guess. Excited. Grateful. Confident. Peaceful."

On the interstate drive back home, I was replaying the whole experience in my mind. What a waste of time, I thought.

But then I started thinking about that sequence where he asked me to imagine there was a miracle. I was replaying my answers. And then something hit me: *Wait a minute. Did I just tell him that if my life was perfect, then I would be happy?*

Because that is exactly what I described—a perfect life. Perfect relationship. Perfect career. Perfect finances. Perfect kid.

Who wouldn't be happy in that case? That's not child*like* but child*ish*. We've learned this lesson already.

But how easily we slip into that trap, don't we? The trap of waiting for one day, someday, when everything is just the way we want it to be. We could say that would truly be a miracle, but really, it's fantasy. There is no such thing.

I remember hearing about the illusion of having it "all together" at a conference I went to one time. That, and the idea that everyone else has it "all together." Except you. Except me.

I knew from my training in mindfulness, psychology, and coaching that I didn't have to wait for my circumstances to be perfect for me to be happy. I knew that I had the power to create my experience by using my Three Tools of Creation—shifting my focus, thoughts, and behavior. In a moment's notice, I could create a different experience.

But, we have this if/then law. If *this* happens, *then* I will be thriving, *then* I will feel happy, *then* I will feel loved, *then* I will feel appreciated, whatever it is.

That's subjecting our life to the conditions around us. And aside from the fact that conditions aren't always what we want, have you ever gotten the thing you wanted, only to find that it didn't feel the way you thought it would feel? How often are we going to experience what we want if this is the system we've set up?

Then something else hit me: While I named all these perfect conditions, I also named how I thought those conditions would make me feel: happy, excited, grateful, confident, peaceful.

Ohhh.

So, what I really want to feel is happy, excited, grateful, confident, and peaceful. And I can cultivate those feelings anytime I choose.

That "miracle question"—and the worst therapy session ever—turned out to be not such a waste of time. Actually, it was pretty mind-blowing. I'm grateful for that time, and for that therapist, who guided me through it.

Now it's your turn: Imagine you went to sleep tonight and overnight, while you slept, there was a miracle. When you wake up in the morning, everything in your life is exactly as you would want it to be. What would you need to see to know that there had been a miracle? Make a list of everything.

And now, how would you feel if you were to experience all of that? Write down all the feelings.

How great would it feel to feel all those feelings?

I know the answer: Amazing.

But, knowing that you *can* feel them right now and *feeling* them right now are two different things. I still had more to learn.

How to Get What You Want... Now

Months went by after the realization—or the remembering—that I don't have to wait to experience what I want to experience.

Trying to apply this in real life, especially when you're surrounded by circumstances you find unpleasant, is difficult. If
you find any of the advice in this book challenging to hear,
know that I do, too. This is the path of *Mastering the Moments*,
and mastery requires work.

Knowing that it may take time for our circumstances to
align with what we desire, it's critical that we learn how to
cultivate the experience we desire even now. While our aim is
to do the right thing, right now, and bring about the changes
we seek in our lives, we also want to learn how to experience
what we want to experience even as the circumstances linger.

What I've learned is that even when you can't do anything
about your circumstances—and you can almost always do
more than you think—you're still not powerless. Before you
do anything, there's something even more powerful that you
can choose.

Once again, My Little Guru was central to this lesson...
even though I thought he was part of the problem.

After drilling down further on what I want most, it became
clear that what I really love is peace. I want to be in a peaceful
state. But life doesn't exactly serve up peace in the way that I
might like it all the time. If you're a parent, or if you've spent
much time around kids, you know what I'm talking about.

Back when My Little Guru was seven or eight, we were well
beyond the days of just "riding my bike" and being happy. The
intensity of the joy he experienced on his bike that day, though,
was still present in other areas of his life. He was—and is—a very
spirited boy with a lot of opinions and a strong will. I used to say

he has all the qualities that you would want in a leader, but that will make life hell as a parent.

I love all those qualities about him, but they don't always align with my definition of peace. It was a friend named Ethan who helped me see new possibilities by asking a rather annoying question.

I was at an event in Chicago, and Ethan and I were backstage talking about some of the very things we've talked about in this book. What do you love? What brings you joy? What do you value in life? What's really important to you?

He asked me some of those questions and I said, "Well, I love peace." Like, "I just want peace." Peace feels good—and I could feel it in my body at that moment, like when you think of your favorite food and you can taste it in your mouth.

I then told him about my son, though, and how around him it's hard to feel peace—and I often don't. "I guess I'm going to have to wait until he's out of the house until I can truly experience peace," I said. And I believed it.

But just as quickly as Brody answered me with, "Riding my bike!" my friend said to me, "Are you sure?"

Remember that question that I gave you to challenge your thoughts previously? Well, this is where it came from. As with everything in this book, I've had to "take my medicine" before daring to give it to you.

Don't you hate it when someone challenges your position? They're supposed to just agree with you, right? You say, "I can't feel peace." You want them to say, "Yeah, I know how that feels." To say, "Oh my gosh, that is rough."

That's what I was looking for. But Ethan had the nerve to ask, "Are you sure?"

What kind of friend is that? A *good* one.

A good friend won't just tell you what you want to hear, they'll tell you what you need to hear. And that's what Ethan did. Which left me thinking, *Am I sure? You should come over to my house and check it out. You should see what it's like over here. I'm pretty sure you would see, there is no peace here.*

Before I could formulate any meaningful response, though, we were interrupted and had to go our separate ways. Then I'm just left hanging with this annoying question.

Are you sure?

When we get hung up on an idea, we don't often slow down to question it, do we? We just accept it as fact.

In this case, I had a vision of what I wanted my life to be and what I would have loved to experience, but... I was also certain that it can't happen right now. Maybe later, maybe someday. But definitely not under the present circumstances.

After this event wrapped up in Chicago, I had about a seven-hour drive home. That gave me time to be tormented even further by this question. *Are you sure? Is it true that I have to wait to experience peace?*

Somewhere between Indianapolis and Louisville it hit me. *Wait.*

If my requirement to feel peace means I'm sitting still, there's a cool breeze blowing, I hear birds chirping and the leaves rustling in trees—if this is my picture of peace and this is what I need to feel peace—then how often am I really going to feel peace? It's going to be hard to get there. When all the stars align, then I will feel peace.

Or, what if my vision is more "reasonable"? If the day is crazy with parenting and business and everything else, as long as I can get just 10 minutes where I'll sit still and meditate, then I'll have my peace. That means 10 minutes out of every day, I'll feel peace. If that's the only way to feel peace, that's not very good either.

On top of that, what am I doing? I'm wishing that a nine-year-old boy would act like a 40-something-year-old man? *That's really good, Shawn.*

Do I want my son to just sit and be quiet and still all the time? *Come on, he's a kid. Let him be a kid. Let him jump and be wild and crazy. It's not his job to give me peace. What I need to do is be peace to him.*

Whoa. *Be peace.*

But what would peace even look like in this environment?

It looks like steadiness. If I can be peace in the midst of all the chaos, then not only is that going to feel better to me, because it allows me to feel what I want to feel, but it also means he can be in a moment of rage, and I can stay still and centered and peaceful and respond to that in the appropriate way. That's better for me, and for him.

That's not to say I'm going to walk around like a monk. I'm human. But, in those times when it feels like chaos, what is needed there is peace. If I jump into the chaos, if I participate in the chaos, then we've just escalated the situation.

One of my favorite coaches, Michael Nitti, says, "There's only two ways you can show up: On purpose, or not."

That's what we're really talking about here: how you show up.

But how could I *be* peace in the midst of all the craziness?

Well, if I'm going to be peace, then the right thing, right now is to make some changes in my daily routines. I need to get up early and have some personal time so I can read or journal or meditate. I need to listen to some encouraging words.

Then, not only would it guarantee that I would experience peace, but then I would also bring peace to him and to those around me. I would be able to be an expression of peace or an embodiment of peace.

Whatever it is that you want to feel, it can be cultivated right now. If you want to experience peace, you can use the breathing exercise that we learned previously to bring it about. If you want to feel excitement, you can find something exciting in your life right now, or something you experienced in the past, and dwell on that. See what you saw. Feel what you felt.

Peace, excitement, happiness, love, gratitude—it's all available, before one single circumstance changes.

And, if we are intentional about cultivating those feelings, how might that impact our ability to attract the circumstances that we desire? How might it affect your relationship, your parenting, your work, your finances—everything?

Legendary motivational speaker and business philosopher, Jim Rohn, said, "Success is not something you chase; it's something you attract by the person you become."

Yes.

Be that which you seek.

It takes practice, but you can only start right where you are.

And it will change everything.

Loving Peace, Embracing Conflict

What you most *want* to experience is not always what you *need* to experience in this moment.

You know peace is what I value most. On the Enneagram, I'm a type Four, known as The Individualist, but for a long time I thought I was a type Nine, known as The Peacemaker, because of how much I craved peace. The Peacemaker has a noble sound to it, doesn't it? One who makes peace.

If you dig in a little bit, though, you find that as with anything good, there's always a shadow side. I do like to make peace, but what I really like is to avoid conflict. I'm not exactly sure where this came from, but I wonder if it came from some of my experiences as a child.

As a young boy, I remember that my dad struggled to control his anger. Now that I'm older, I understand that this came from some trauma in his own childhood. He had made significant progress from what he saw as a child, and I'm very thankful that I wasn't subjected to some of the things he was. Through continued work and growth on his part, by the time I got into my adult years, he had made a true transformation.

When I was a kid, though, I can remember him losing his temper and punching holes in the wall or peeling out of our gravel driveway in a fit of anger. Is it possible, then, that having seen this, early on I decided—consciously or unconsciously—that I was better to blend into the background and not cause any conflict?

In the last few years, doing my own inner work, I came to realize that I had developed a belief that conflict is bad. Conflict seemed to be in opposition to peace, so I would do anything to avoid conflict.

I know I'm not alone in wanting to avoid conflict, and I also know that many of us have someone in our lives who seemingly loves to go around creating conflict. So, the idea that "conflict is bad" doesn't seem like a terrible one. The world would be better with a little—or a lot—less conflict.

But, if you have the belief that conflict is bad, it can cause you to shrink and not stand up in places where you should stand up. In my life, I can see where that belief held me back in areas of business, relationships, and even parenting.

I wouldn't say things I needed to say.

I wouldn't stand up for my own needs.

I wouldn't hold boundaries where I needed to.

The thing is, while avoiding conflict *feels* like peace on the surface, in reality, it causes great turmoil. You walk around feeling like you're getting run over. You walk around with your needs unmet. You walk around feeling like no one knows who you really are. And we all want to be seen and known. That's another way of saying, we all want to be loved. But we can't be fully loved if we aren't allowing ourselves to be fully seen.

But, to allow yourself to be fully seen means there will be conflict.

You *will* say something someone doesn't agree with.

You *will* act in ways that others don't appreciate.

You *will* rub people the wrong way.

And that's okay.

As a matter of fact, what I came to realize is that conflict is not bad. Conflict is the path to growth. At least, it opens the door to the possibility for growth.

If, as a speaker, I show up and only say things you agree with, it will feel good—to you—but there will be no growth. You will also lose interest at some point. *I already know all of this. Why am I listening?*

If I show up and say what I believe, and you show up and say what you believe, even if we are opposed to one another, as long as we are open to the other person's point of view, we can both walk away from the encounter richer and wiser than we were when we went into it.

Of course, you never control how someone will show up, but you do control how you show up. I control how I show up. And my responsibility is to show up and say what is true for me. (That's not a license to show up arrogantly. It's simply a license to speak your truth and honor your experience.)

I remember after time, after I had let go of the belief that conflict is bad and I was working on embracing the belief that conflict is the path to growth, I had a rather heated exchange with my landlord.

He was a retired gentleman, and he was quite particular about the way he wanted his yard landscaped. He wanted the hedges to be trimmed—and kept—at the same height as the fence. If it were his property and he were living there, then of course he would be entitled to do it however he wants to do it. The problem was, as a single dad trying to keep up with the demands of parenting a neurodivergent child and rebuilding a business, I had other priorities.

The best way I've found to keep up with all the things and not lose my sanity is by using the "Take a Number" system I shared previously. Knowing I can only get done what I can get done, I assign all my tasks a number. Trimming the hedges regularly was low on my list, but seemingly always next-up on his. I hated every time he asked me about those damn hedges.

For a long time, I had tried to avoid conflict and just pacify him from one encounter to the next. This was still letting him encroach on my boundaries, though. Finally, the day came when I had had enough. We stood in the front yard, and I told him exactly what I thought—kindly yet firmly. I told him that his expectations were unrealistic and inappropriate.

He disagreed and left quite unhappy. My heart was racing. I wondered if I had just set myself up for a lot of misery moving forward. He was a kind man, we just disagreed about the hedges (and a few other things as it relates to landlord-tenant responsibilities). I hated that feeling.

Simultaneously, I was proud of myself for standing my ground. For the first time in this space, I felt true peace. Not peace that came from the absence of conflict. Peace that came from me being fully me. Whatever the landlord did, I knew I had honored myself.

This is a key element of *Mastering the Moments*. It's about so much more than just being present. It's about you and I living lives that are in full alignment with who we truly are. That's when you experience true peace and joy and love.

It will require us to get uncomfortable at times, though. It will require us to examine our beliefs, and perhaps let go of those which no longer serve us.

As a child, believing that "conflict is bad" was a survival mechanism. It kept me safe, physically. As an adult, though, holding to that old belief was like death to my soul.

This is why we must be willing to embrace something that is temporarily uncomfortable in order to experience the ultimate demonstration of what we truly desire.

I'm curious: Have any old, worn-out beliefs which are no longer serving you come to mind while reading about my experience? Like my belief that "conflict is bad," is there a belief you're holding on to which is holding you back from living a fully aligned life?

Philosopher Alan Watts said, "You're under no obligation to be the same person you were five minutes ago." You can let those old beliefs go and adopt new ones.

By the way, the next time my landlord and I saw each other, everything was cordial. There was no lingering animosity. It was an "aha" moment for me as I realized, *Oh, I can stand firm, engage in conflict, and we can still be "good."* It's part of growing up... which sometimes happens when we are already grown-ups.

Also, he never did bother me about the landscaping again.

Four C's That Crush a Creator

Beyond the unique beliefs that each of us hold, which have held us back, there are some "built-in" obstacles to embracing our true selves and honoring our desires that are common to all of us.

In Ralph Waldo Emerson's essay, *Self-Reliance*, he identifies conformity, comparison, and consistency as three critical barriers to us living authentically. When I finally read this classic work,

I realized just how much they had influenced my own life decisions.

It's worth highlighting each of them here—along with one more I'll add—so you can see if or how they've been shaping yours, as well. I call them the Four C's that Crush a Creator.

Conformity is about trying to fit into the mold that society, family, or friends have created for you. It's about living up to others' expectations and standards rather than your own. Which means it's also about feeding others' happiness rather than your own.

As a youngster, I marched to the beat of my own drum. For example, my high school attire often included wildly colorful shirts—many made of rayon—and red Chuck Taylors. Then when graduation came, I shunned a suit and wore jeans and Caterpillar work boots.

Somewhere along the way, though, I found comfort in the safety of conformity. It wasn't until a few years ago that I wrote proudly in my journal, "I'm weird." I don't think this was news to anyone who knew me well, but it was time for me to embrace it myself.

"I've always been a weirdo," I continued, "living in a world that doesn't like weirdos."

Indeed, the world likes conformity. It's what we're taught at a young age. We go to school and when the bell rings, you sit down, shut up, and do what you're told. Before you know it, it's just how you live.

Mastering the Moments is about waking up to who you truly are, though.

What would you do if you didn't care what people thought?

It's okay to be weird. I'll be right next to you.

Comparison is the thief of joy. It has you constantly measuring your journey against others and leaves you feeling inadequate if you don't measure up. Comparing yourself to others never produces true happiness, though. This is *your* journey. It doesn't matter how it compares to others.

Martha Beck points out in her book, *Finding Your Own North Star*, that Moses never reached the promised land. If we're comparing him to others who reached their goal, then his journey failed. But, as Martha says, "Maybe Moses was a voyager, born to thrive in the wilderness, not interested in a stable, uneventful life."

I love that.

My journey is certainly not a success in some others' eyes. And that's okay. I'm not doing it for them. I'm not trying to be better than them. I just want to keep getting better for myself. If I am, that's success.

What about you?

Consistency refers to the belief that you must always remain the same. Remember what I said about your identity being the hardest thing to break free from? How you've done things in the past is irrelevant. That Alan Watts line bears repeating: "You are under no obligation to be the same person you were five minutes ago." You have the right to change, grow, and evolve—unless you're a politician. Then, apparently, you must hold the same views for your lifetime.

Adaptability is a key demonstration of *Mastering the Moments*. Are you allowing yourself that freedom?

Capability is the fourth C I will add here. It's a voice that has shown up often on my journey, saying, "You don't know how to do that." It causes you to doubt your abilities and potential. It calls you back to your comfort zone.

When your vision tells you it's time to rise to the next level, it will surely call you beyond your current capabilities. Even if you've become comfortable and complacent, you can grow again. Look back to when you were in kindergarten, to now. You have a track record of growing and changing.

Don't ask yourself if you *can* do the thing you feel called to do. Ask yourself what capabilities you need to upgrade in pursuit of that vision.

When you find one of these four voices pulling you back, know that they are not your highest, best self. They're not *you*. If anything, they're your ego, trying to keep you safe—from embarrassment from others, or from disappointing yourself.

The first two will have you setting your vision based on other people—and their journey is not yours. The last two will have you setting your vision based on your present (what you can do right now) or your past (what you have done previously).

Perhaps these are the voices that have guided your life up to this point. In that case, this idea of catching a vision for the next chapter of your life may be a foreign or uncomfortable one. That's okay. One moment at a time, remember?

Mastering the Moments is about living a life of authenticity. Each step of the way, remember to embrace your weirdness, stop comparing your journey to others, allow yourself to change and grow, and trust in your capability to rise to the next level.

I've got a tool that might help you in the process...

Would You Rather...?

Once we gain an understanding of what we really want and learn how to be that which we seek in this moment—even if it means embracing conflict and overcoming the barriers of conformity, comparison, consistency, and capability—we are on the path toward living authentically and embracing our true desires.

Then we come back to the question: *What is the right thing, right now?*

Let me share an experience to illustrate the power of *being* before *doing*, and then I'll share a simple tool—a game, really—to help you do this with greater ease and consistency.

A few years ago, I almost bought a Land Rover. For many years, I had a Land Rover on my vision board. It's not the leather or the luxury, but the "go anywhere" offroad prowess that I love.

A while after things had turned around dramatically in my business, I found one in the price range I was comfortable with and went to take it for a test drive. It was perfect. The payment was doable. It felt like it was "my time."

Sitting there at the dealership, pen in hand, one signature away from owning my dream car, something in my gut said it wasn't right. I had finally gotten out of debt, and now I was about to go back in again? That didn't feel good. My stomach churning, I realized I was out of alignment with what I truly valued. So, I did the hard thing and told the salesman I had changed my mind.

The next day, while out running errands in my old, 200,000-mile, fully paid-off Mazda, I pulled up to stop sign with a sense of pride and freedom. Alignment feels *good*.

Then while driving around, something else came to my mind. I remembered that just two years prior, I had considered joining a boutique gym with a personal trainer for about the same price—but I couldn't afford it at the time. Now, I could. Sometimes—or often—we'll invest the same amount in a "thing" that we would say is too much to invest in ourselves.

At that time, I had been reciting a daily affirmation, "I'm growing happier, healthier, stronger, and wealthier with every passing day," for months. Affirmations don't inherently "make" things happen, but they keep your mind focused on what you desire. When spoken with feeling—a feeling that's congruent with the words—they help you *be that which you seek.*

Buying a Land Rover wouldn't make me happier, healthier, stronger, and wealthier with every passing day, but investing in a gym and personal trainer would. So, I chose to join the gym, aligning my actions with my true desires.

Over the next year, I got in the best shape of my life. I never regretted my monthly investment in myself, but very likely, at some point I would have regretted my decision to buy a Land Rover. As a matter of fact—because the Universe is hilarious—there was a woman at the gym who drove a Land Rover almost identical to the one I almost bought. On a regular basis she cursed how unreliable it was and couldn't wait to sell it.

Here's the question I could have asked myself to save all the drama:

Would you rather buy a Land Rover and face the financial stress and regret of being out of alignment with your true desires? Or would you rather drive your reliable old car, invest in a gym membership, and

experience the long-term benefits of being in the best shape of your
life, feeling strong, healthy, and truly aligned with who you want to
be?

You might recognize that this is a twist on the popular conversational game, "Would you rather…"

I remember the first time I played it. I was doing some contract work on a team with about a half dozen other guys. One day we were standing around the kitchen island eating lunch and one of the guys kicked it off with, "Would you rather be attacked by a hundred ducks or one hippopotamus?"

What?!

I'm an introvert, remember? I'm selective about talking to people anyway, but to banter about over a nonsense hypothetical? How can you make decisions of this magnitude on the fly, anyway? You call this a *game*? Being a team player, though, I joined in. And I survived.

While I'm not a fan of the game, I am always looking for tools that can support us on the journey of *Mastering the Moments*. I discovered there's a way we can make this silly game work for us. In a powerful way.

If you notice the wording of my "Would you rather…?" Land Rover scenario above, it doesn't just ask, "Would you rather do what's uncomfortable now or do what feels good now?" No one in their right mind is going to choose what's uncomfortable over what feels good. I'll take "what feels good" for $1,000, Alex.

It asks, "Would you rather do what's uncomfortable now *and enjoy the long-term gains*, or do what feels good now *and suffer the long-term consequences*?" And when we add in those extra phrases—"enjoy the long-term gains" or "suffer the long-term consequences"—it forces our brain to think differently, and it also gives it a sense of autonomy.

From a neuroscience perspective, thinking about the long-term gains and consequences activates parts of the brain associated with long-term planning and reward systems. In contrast, our default is "survival mode," which only asks: What is the safest—or most comfortable—route right now?

When we choose paths aligned with our deeper values, we bypass the need for sheer willpower to make the "right" decision and instead engage more sustainable, intrinsic motivation. The more often we do this, the more we rewire our brains to support habits that lead to lasting fulfillment rather than transient pleasure. Truly, moments create momentum.

The next time you're faced with a decision—or a temptation—to do what's familiar and comfortable or do what's right but uncomfortable, ask yourself:

> *Would you rather [take the safe and familiar route in this moment yet experience the pain and disappointment and resentment and other side effects of that choice for a long time to come]? Or would you rather [do what is uncomfortable in the moment, yet you know is fully aligned with who you are and the life you want to live, allowing you to feel true peace for a long time to come, while also moving you closer to experiencing the outcomes you desire]?*

The right thing, right now might come easier than you expect.

Chapter 6

Relax, Let Go, and Trust

Don't Worry If It Doesn't Look Like Anything Yet

As we continue on this journey of *Mastering the Moments*, it's important to address a common misconception, that progress is always visible and linear. To the contrary, it's possible to have made tremendous progress, only to look around and wonder, *Am I any better off at all?* You might even think, *It feels like I'm moving backwards.*

These are the spots where we're often tempted to give up. I know I was. Yet the truth is, the only way to fail on this journey is if you *do* give up.

It reminds me of an old Zen saying Elmo shared with us during mindfulness class: "Better not to start. Once started, better to finish."

Truly, in some ways, it would be easier to be ignorant to much of what we've talked about so far. Just coast through life, take what it gives you, and "run out the clock" till the game is over. If you do decide to dive in, listen to your heart, and pursue those divine desires, though, it's better to see it through. As tough as it is, the rewards are like nothing else.

What you must know, though, is that once you begin the process of turning your life around, you never know how long the "old," undesirable circumstances are going to linger. You also never know how long the ultimate change you seek is going to take. What you must do, though, is keep going. Even when the circumstances tell you otherwise.

For a vivid demonstration of this truth, let's go to a painting workshop I attended with Steve Ross, son of the beloved Bob Ross, and Dana Jester, a dear friend of Bob.

I don't know about you, but I love watching Bob Ross. Not only are his paintings beautiful, but he just always seems to know the right thing to say.

"You need the dark to show the light."

"There are no mistakes, just happy accidents."

"You can do anything you want. This is your world."

"The secret to doing anything is believing that you can do it."

"Beat the devil out of it." (Okay, that one's not so profound but it's a classic.)

I used to think, *I wish I could have learned to paint from Bob Ross.* Of course, he's been gone for almost 30 years, so I knew that wasn't possible. I figured watching *The Joy of Painting* was as close as I would get—and thank goodness for reruns of *The Joy of Painting.*

At one point, I tried to track down Bob's son, Steve, who had been a guest painter on *The Joy of Painting* a few times. It seemed he had gone into hiding, though. Until a few years ago, when I started seeing posts on Instagram about Steve and Dana doing a series of painting workshops. OMG!!!

I watched the posts as they announced new workshops in Colorado, Indiana, Florida, and other locations. Then, one day, I saw what I had been looking for: Tennessee. There was going to be a workshop in Tennessee! It was about three hours from where I lived in Nashville, but there was no question. I had to be there. When life serves up opportunities, your job is to say *yes!*

I was so excited to go to this workshop. I would finally get to put Bob's promise to the test. "You can do it!" he had told me many times through the screen. And I believed him.

When Dana and Steve sent out a list of necessary supplies, I ordered my two-inch brush and some of the familiar colors that I had seen run across the bottom of the screen so many times. I also ordered my easel—I mean, I had nothing. This was my first time painting since messing around with Brody's watercolors.

What I didn't know is that for painting workshops, attendees usually bring a tabletop easel. Having never been to a painting workshop, though, I bought a large studio-sized easel not so different from what Bob used on the show. When I walked into the classroom and saw everyone seated at tables in rows, I knew I was in trouble.

Shy Shawn would have probably turned and walked out right then, but I was there to learn to paint, dammit, so I set up at the back of the room and I was ready to go.

As we were getting started, Steve told us which colors of paint to set up on our palette. We took our pre-stretched 18-by-24 canvas and put on a light coat of Liquid White. Boy, I felt just like Bob.

When I told Steve I had always wanted to do this, he said, "Well, you've got the beard for it." The dry, witty sense of humor clearly runs in the family.

After adding the Liquid White, it was time to get started on the actual painting. We started by painting what would be a hot pink sky, mirrored in the reflection in the water. Then we added some deep blue onto the corners—also reflecting in the water. If you've watched *The Joy of Painting*, you know how this works.

We were about 30 minutes when I looked down at my canvas and... I was not feeling so much like Bob anymore.

With a mighty two-inch brush in hand and Bob's promise that I could do it in my mind, I felt so confident. But now, what I saw on my canvas was a *mess*. All the confidence had drained out of my body and what I was experiencing was *not* the joy of painting. More like, the misery of painting.

"You can do it," Bob told us so many times through the TV screen. *I want to quit* is what I was thinking, though. *Maybe Bob is a liar.*

As if right on cue, it was at about that time that Steve said to the entire room, "Don't worry if it doesn't look like anything yet."

Oh, so this is normal.

I mustered up the courage to keep going.

Reflecting on that experience, though, it takes me back to a time when my *life* didn't look like anything yet.

It was the summer of 2017. I'll never forget it. I was standing in the kitchen of my two-bedroom apartment where I was living, recently divorced, with my five-year-old son. I had taken the courageous steps to move across town in pursuit of the "better life" my mentor said I was not wrong to want... but this was not what I had in mind.

I was standing in my kitchen, having just walked out of my office—which, between you and me, was a converted closet—where I had been running some numbers for myself and the business. Taking inventory of the money in the accounts, the money that was due to me, and the money that I was due to pay, I realized it didn't look good. *I'm scared*, I said to myself.

I remember it well because it was the first time I had said those words to myself: I'm scared. I don't know about you, but as an entrepreneur, leader, or achiever, we don't often say we're "scared." We'll say, "I'm stressed. It's pretty tough. It's hard. I'm feeling some pressure"—the same kind of "pressure" the dentist warns you about, which we all know is pain!

Whereas I needed my mentor's honest assessment a few years ago, this time, I was honest with myself. I knew it wasn't good, because at that time, we were still recovering from the Great Recession. Now here I am, a single dad trying to support two households. Bill collectors were calling me every day, and I wasn't answering.

Indeed, it didn't look like anything yet. It was a mess.

After feeling the fear, though, my next thought was, *I shouldn't be here.*

As I told you previously, I had played by the rules. Went to bed early. Got up early. Did my homework. Made the Honor Roll. Ate my vegetables. You know, everything they tell you to do to achieve "success." Ugh. *I'm not the one who's supposed to be in this situation.*

The pity party was in full swing.

To state the obvious, nothing we've learned on the journey of *Mastering the Moments* makes you immune to challenges. It doesn't mean you'll never feel anxious or scared or angry again. It also doesn't mean that just because you *know* to be peace that you *will* always be peace.

The simple truth is that growth is a non-linear path often filled with setbacks, where old fears and habits resurface even after breakthrough realizations. This is the human experience.

It's also worth noting that, just as I found the courage to take the steps toward building my ideal business *before* I got the nerve to tackle my relationship, here I had some new perspective on my parenting but was still struggling in the financial department. There are multiple spheres of life—finances, career, health, relationships, etc.—and they don't all come together simultaneously.

Maybe you give yourself an A in career and finances but a D in health and a C in relationships right now. You decide to place an emphasis on your health and you bring that up to a B over the next six months. In the midst of it, though, you get laid off and your career drops to a C. Now you have to divert more time and resources back to that area.

Life is never "all good" or "all bad." It's always a mixed bag. It's a dynamic operation. Give yourself grace as you navigate through it all.

My pity party was soon interrupted by a new thought: *What do you mean, you shouldn't be here?* That one was quickly followed by, *You think you're too good for this?*

I had my own little coaching session right there in my kitchen.

No, of course I'm not too good for this. I know, it can happen to anyone.

Really, it does happen to everyone.

We all end up in these spaces from time to time.

Then, *I'm actually right where I should be. I made all the choices that brought me here.*

No, I didn't make my spouse's choices. I didn't choose the Great Recession. Lots of things I didn't choose, but I chose to get into that marriage. I chose the conversations to have or not have. I chose my business. I chose how I had structured my business and what I did with my money. I made all those choices... which brought me right. here.

These thoughts opened the door to the next one: *Wait a minute. Yes, I am here, and it's not where I want to be, but look how far I've come.*

While we achievers don't often admit fear, we also don't often look back to see how far we've come. That's because we're too busy looking ahead to that grand vision we're chasing... and fretting about how far we have to go.

When I paused to look back, I realized, *Whoa, I'm no longer in an unhealthy marriage. I'm doing work I love. I'm so much better off than I used to be. No, things aren't where I want them to be, but I'm making different choices now. I'm looking at life differently.*

Remember, sometimes the change takes longer than you think. Sometimes the circumstances linger longer than you expect. But if you're no longer making the choices you used to make, then you are truly on a different path. Those present circumstances may just be the residue from past decisions. Let me say that again: Those present circumstances may just be the residue from past decisions.

After ditching my pity party and celebrating how far I had come, I was feeling better. Remember, it's not the *moments* that shape us, but how *we* shape the moments, that defines our lives. I had claimed my power to transform my experience, leveraging some of the tools I had learned years before.

Building on the momentum of that moment, I remembered a lesson I had learned from Tony Robbins.

Tony teaches something he calls Transformational Vocabulary. The essence is, by changing the language we use to describe our experiences, we can significantly alter our emotional and mental states.

This works both to amplify positive experiences and to take the edge off negative ones. For example, instead of describing a really great day as being "pretty good," we can say, "I'm really grateful," which has more feeling to it. Likewise, saying, "I'm exhausted," when you're feeling tired is likely to drain your energy even further, compared to something like, "I could use some rest."

Remembering this, I decided to try an experiment.

I said I was "scared" due to my present financial circumstances. That was true. I was. "Scared" is an intense word, though. It has a certain emotional identity that comes with it. Tense. Cowered. Weak. Doomed.

Recognizing this, I thought to myself, *What's another way to describe the experience that has a little less charge to it?* I don't want to deny the reality of the experience, but I also don't want to amplify the feeling of it.

"Concerned" is the word that came to mind.

I'm concerned.

That acknowledges that this really doesn't look good, and there could be some danger up ahead, but I'm *concerned* about it rather than actively *scared* of it. It's like a cautionary road sign that says, "Curve ahead, slow down." That felt better. Not so catastrophic.

As a matter of fact, it felt so much better that I wondered if I could even take it a step further. *Is there another word that would honor the reality yet have even less intensity?*

The word "curious" popped into my head.

I'm curious.

Again, not denying the present reality, but a very different way to look at it. There is uncertainty ahead. I'm not sure what's going to happen. *I'm curious how this is going to turn out.*

All of a sudden, it felt like I was watching a great adventure movie. Let me pop some popcorn and see how this is going to turn out!

The power of Transformative Vocabulary is real.

Even though the circumstances didn't look like anything yet, I kept going.

Look for Signs

Curious is exactly what I was when days after my pity party, I received a message on LinkedIn inviting me to speak at a west Nashville Chamber of Commerce event. It was the first time I had received a speaking invitation via a LinkedIn message, so it was especially memorable.

A man named Doug reached out and said, "I came across your info on LinkedIn and believe our members would welcome an opportunity to hear you speak to topics that could help them grow their business. Wondering if you would be interested in talking to our west Nashville group?"

Funny thing is, I had been to one of this Chamber's meetings more than a decade prior. Vanderbilt University's baseball head coach, Tim Corbin, had been the speaker and I remember thinking, "This guy is really good!" It was no surprise, then, when a decade later he led Vanderbilt to a national championship—their first of two in the last 10 seasons.

Upon further research, I found that the Chamber's most recent speaker had been the General Manager of the Tennessee Titans... which made me think, *do you have the right guy?*

Turns out they did, and a few weeks later, we firmed up plans for me to speak at one of their breakfasts. There's nothing remarkable about this story until I receive an email from Doug with the logistical details of the program. He wrote:

"The location of the event is 1234 Sawyer Brown Rd., Nashville TN."

That's not the actual street number. But that is the actual road. *Sawyer Brown Road.*

If you read the Introduction—you didn't skip it, did you?!—then you read about how being at a Sawyer Brown concert when I was nine years old inspired me to play piano, which ultimately led to me moving to Nashville to pursue a career in music. There's a lot more to the "Sawyer Brown story," though.

Before we ever got to the concert, I remember a moment when I was sitting in front of the TV with my little brother, Kirk. I was nine years old. Kirk was three. We were watching PBS.

I don't remember exactly what we were watching—maybe *Sesame Street* or *Mister Rogers' Neighborhood*—but I do remember a promo that came on. The promo was for a show called *Austin City Limits*. One of the featured acts on that week's episode was a band called Sawyer Brown.

From across the room, my parents recognized one of the songs—"Hey, that's the song we've been hearing on the radio! We need to watch!" (The song was "Leona," by the way.)

When Saturday night rolled around and *Austin City Limits* came on, my parents claimed the TV. I wasn't too happy about that. I can remember protesting by sitting near the top of our steps—adjacent to the TV—and watching through the banister, which my dad had constructed of 2x4s.

While I couldn't admit it at the time, I thought this band was pretty cool. We all did, and a few months later, we went to see Sawyer Brown in-person.

They were playing at a county fair a couple of hours away from us. We made the drive, found our way to the entertainment area of the fairgrounds, and set up our lawn chairs about 30 rows back.

We waited with anticipation for the concert to start and as soon as it did, I was hooked. I had never seen energy like that on stage, and for whatever reason, I was especially captivated by the keyboard player.

I don't know why the keyboard player got my attention rather than the lead singer or drummer or lead guitarist. But Hobie, bouncing around on his stool, smiling, is the one I was drawn to. So much so that I went home and all I wanted to do was play piano. Except, we didn't have a piano. So, the oven handle of our kitchen stove would have to do.

I would play along through one side our Sawyer Brown cassette tape, flip it over, and go again, bouncing and feeling the music just like Hobie. All along the way, I begged my parents for piano lessons, and after a couple of years, they finally gave in. (Actually, looking back on it now, I wonder if it just took a couple of years for them to have money to pay for piano lessons.)

I wasn't a very athletic kid growing up. Maybe I should say I wasn't a very coordinated kid growing up. And I was pretty scrawny, having started school when I was still four years old. In a lot of ways, then, compared to my peers, I felt inadequate. In playing piano, though, I found something I loved, and I was actually good at it.

We kept going to see Sawyer Brown concerts as a family—probably three or four times a year. If they came within a three-hour radius of our home, we were there. My love for music continued to grow, the point I decided I wanted to pursue that as my career.

First, though, I would go to college.

Sawyer Brown's drummer, Joe, had gone to Berklee College of Music in Boston—I knew that from his bio—so I figured that would be a good place for me, too. That was my plan, until one night, at another Sawyer Brown concert, there was another meaningful moment.

The lead singer, Mark, came out for the encore wearing a t-shirt for some school I had never heard of: Belmont University. I looked it up—and this was before the days of the internet, so that probably meant going to the library and checking out a directory of colleges—and learned that it was in Nashville. I also learned that the school had the most renowned music business program in the country.

I applied to attend, I was accepted, and with hopes and dreams, I moved to Nashville in 1994.

Now, you've already heard about my failed audition with Lee Greenwood, and the fact you're reading my book rather than listening to my latest single is further evidence that things didn't go quite according to plan. And yet, if I hadn't gone to Belmont, which led to me getting a job for a speaker booking agency, which put thoughts of this wild and crazy career path in my head, there may not be a *Mastering the Moments* book to read.

- But I would have never known about Belmont if Mark hadn't decided to wear that shirt that night...

- Which, of course, I never would have seen if we hadn't been at that concert...

- Which we likely *wouldn't* have been at if we hadn't gone to that first one...

- And we would have never gone to that first one had we not watched Sawyer Brown on *Austin City Limits*...

- Which, of course, we would have missed if my brother and I hadn't had the TV tuned to PBS that afternoon.

All of this came flooding through my mind when I saw where I was going to be speaking. When I was a kid, I wrote letters to Hobie asking to go *on the road* with Sawyer Brown. Now, here I was, about to speak *on Sawyer Brown Road*.

God, you're still not getting these prayers right! I thought.

If not for Sawyer Brown, much of my life may not have unfolded as it did.

It's funny how such tiny moments can set a course in motion. It's also funny when, over 30 years later, long after my music dreams have faded, it's as if Life winked at me, hinting that there is something else going on here. For years, I had been planning, pushing, and fighting to achieve success, yet looking back, all these little "Sawyer Brown moments" seemed to guide me here.

Long before I met Steve Ross, it's like the Universe itself was saying, "Don't worry if it doesn't look like anything yet." I thought, *I shouldn't be here*, but it felt as if the Universe sent me a sign—literally—to affirm, "You're exactly where you're supposed to be."

You may or may not agree with that, and that's okay. Remember, it's not the moments that have shaped us, but how we shape the moments, that defines our lives. It's what we take out of those moments. And I took a *lot* out of this one.

Have you ever retraced your steps to see exactly what started you on the path that got you to where you are today?

We set our goals, make our plans, and fight and push and strive to "make it happen," but then it seems the most beautiful things in life just come as gifts.

We get so worked up—at least I do—trying to control everything, but the truth is, there are only two things that are truly in our control: how we show up, and how we respond, moment by moment.

Seeing this "sign," I thought, *Maybe I should just relax a little bit. Maybe I should let go a little bit. And trust the process.*

When I finally spoke at that Chamber event, I shared this story and asked this question:

"When it seems like *nothing* has gone according to plan, what if it's *all* according to plan?"

What I mean by that is, what if all of life has been designed to help you become the best of who you are, to live the life that you know you're here to live? I realize it can be a big leap to consider that possibility amid life's challenges, though. So, how do you keep going in those spaces where everything around you says you should give up or turn and run?

Look for signs. Even when things don't look good, look for signs that tell you you're on the right track. Maybe it's a literal sign like "Sawyer Brown Road," or maybe it's something more symbolic that speaks to you.

Have you ever seen a cardinal glide in and land on a tree limb? Or in the grass in front of you? Some say cardinals are signs that you are not alone, and that your loved ones or angels are near to protect, bless, and guide you. Some say that if you see a cardinal after the death of a loved one, it is letting you know that they have made it home. When I see a cardinal in my backyard, I think of my grandma and grandpa and other loved ones who have transitioned to the other side, and I wonder if the red bird is reminding me that they're watching over me.

In recent years, I've come to pay close attention to numbers—or more like, numbers have come to grab my attention.

Prior to the pandemic, I noticed that I started seeing the time 11:11 on the clock frequently—both morning and night. It was strange how often I would see this time—more than any other time. After a quick Google search, I read that seeing the number 1111 can mean that you're on the right path, connecting with your intuition, or that your guardian angel is close.

You have the choice to disregard all that, or embrace it. I choose to embrace it, and I'm comforted every time I see 11:11—whether on a clock, or elsewhere "in the wild." One time, I was on a date with a woman and we walked by a house with the number 1111. I asked if she knew about the meaning of 1111 and she didn't. That was a sign she wasn't the one for me. (One of them, at least.)

When I moved to Ohio a year ago, my apartment number was 808. That didn't strike me as anything meaningful, until I started seeing 8:08 on the clock morning and night—so much so that it registered as "interesting." Again, I looked it up to see what it might mean. This time, I read that in numerology, the number 808 is associated with prosperity and abundance. It's believed to represent wealth, peace, harmony, and balance. It may also signal that you're on the brink of spiritual rebirth.

I've been seeing that number for more than a year now, sometimes in the strangest of places. One day recently, I turned on the TV and an NBA game was on. Gameplay was stopped at... you guessed it. 8:08.

Is that just a random thing? Or, is it the Universe giving me a sign that I'm on the right track? As always, it is as you believe.

Here's my favorite number of the past year, though: 23.

Again, when I moved to Ohio, I noticed it showing up everywhere. First, my apartment complex was off of highway 23. My exit off the interstate was exit 23. The year, by the way, was 2023. It was a major shift in my life, leaving Nashville where I had moved to almost 30 years prior to pursue my dreams, and the signs seemed to keep assuring me I was on the right track.

Then, when I went to get my new license plates in Ohio, the cashier went to get my new plate off the stack and when she brought me mine, the last two digits on the plate were... 23.

What I had initially missed—oddly—was that my birthday is also the 23rd day of the month. Twenty-three is seemingly "my number."

You may think all my signs are crazy, and that's absolutely fine. Here's the thing about signs: they only need to matter to you, because they're for you. It doesn't matter how small it is, or how strange it is.

Want to see more signs in your life? Look for them. Be open to them. See if something starts showing up in an oddly frequent way. See if something strange shows up.

Here's the thing, though. Seeing signs—getting confirmation you're on the right track—doesn't guarantee it will all be smooth sailing. That's why you need something more.

Create Your "Faith File"

We must trust the process, remember? But, there is no need to trust when everything is going smoothly. Trust, or faith, is exercised when the circumstances around you are in opposition to what you would expect or desire.

While I learned about one aspect of faith while watching televangelists with my grandma, I learned something else about faith from farming with my grandpa as a kid.

I told you I grew up three miles down a dirt road, and a mile further down that dirt road lived my grandparents. They were semi-retired farmers by the time I came along, but I still have a lot of memories of bailing hay, tending to the cows, and raising crops with my grandpa. He was my hero growing up. A simple man—who thought 55 should be the maximum speed limit anywhere—who no one knew, but he was the rock of his family.

I remember one time, after a day of planting crops, we had put the little tractor in the shed—no big, fancy, air-conditioned cab tractors for him—and we were walking back across the road to the house. As we walked, Grandpa said, "I've done my part, and now it's up to the good man up above."

Whatever your belief is, whether you believe it's the good man, good woman, source, spirit, universe, or nature, the reality is the same: once you plant a seed in the soil, it's in the dark. It's out of your control. You can fertilize the soil, cultivate it, and clear the weeds, but ultimately, that seed is going to sprout—or not—as it's designed to do.

What my grandpa was saying, in effect, was "I've done my best, and now it's time to rest."

Or, relax, let go, and trust the process. Even if it doesn't look like anything yet.

It's funny how you can *hear* something or *learn* something in one phase of life, but then later you have a real *experience* that allows you to truly *understand* it.

How do you trust, though, when everything around you says you shouldn't?

Well, by the time I heard my grandpa say those words, he had been farming for over 50 years of his life. He knew that this is how it worked. He had seen it time and time again.

How did Steve know to say, "Don't worry if it doesn't look like anything yet"? He had never seen me—or anyone else in the class—paint. Why shouldn't I be *really* worried?!

Steve knew because he had seen all of this play out thousands of times before. He knew that every painting—especially when you're just starting out—goes through a phase where it doesn't look like anything yet. And isn't that true of every major undertaking in life?

Think about relationships. Think about parenting.

There is always a point where you think, *Ugh, this looks like a huge mistake. I have royally screwed this up.* And, often times, that's where we turn and run. Frankly, this is one of the lessons it took me a long time learn in life.

On multiple occasions, I gave up or quit at the first sign of difficulty, rather than pressing through to the other side. I quit Tae Kwon Do. I quit my 5th grade basketball team. I quit my first job. Who knows what might have been possible had I kept going. I don't have any regrets today, but I do know that I didn't reach my full potential in any of those spaces.

Today, I make it a point to persist.

Your *will* will only take you so far, though.

Look at your past to find solid evidence you can lean on.

If I had published this book when I initially intended to publish it, about five years ago, it would have been a picture-perfect fairytale ending. Bankrupt to best year ever. And... *scene.* Fade to black. Beautiful. Perfect.

You and I both know "perfect" is not how life goes, though.

It was just a few months after celebrating our best year ever that I was walking in Los Angeles and I came to that END sign.

The one where I said, "It looks more like a beginning to me." Remember?

That was less than a year before the entire world would shut down due to the global pandemic. In a one-week period, we had our first even cancellation, my girlfriend decided she wanted to see other people, and I found out that my dog, Lucy's, cancer was back, and it was inoperable.

END.

Just two short years after two great years, my whole business was turned upside down. Our business was built on live events with large gatherings of people, and all of a sudden there were no live events with large gatherings of people. 2020 did *not* set a new record for our best year ever.

What struck me, though, was that during all of this, I never had the thought, *Here we go again.* That would be a very easy thought to have. That's what I had thought when my plans or vision had been derailed in the past.

During the Great Recession I was afraid, I was mad, I was angry, I was sad. During the global pandemic—which was even more devastating—I found myself hopeful and even excited at times. Not by what I *saw*, but by what I *knew*. Because this time, I could look back on my past experience and find strength. I could look back on my past experience and find hope. I didn't need a motivational speaker or a book to pick me up. I just had to look at my own story. And you can do the same.

This book is largely a collection of my stories, and one reason I tell these stories is because they happen to be the ones I know the best. The other reason I share them, though, is because I know that when I share *my* story, you'll find *your* story.

Where have you experienced a turnaround in your life? It doesn't matter how big or how small it is. What is a difficult situation you faced in the past—one that was especially intimidating to you—that you have now overcome or moved beyond?

Where have you come to a place that you thought you wouldn't get through, and not only did you get through it, but something even better came on the other side of it? What did you learn about yourself in that process?

Remember *those* stories—those experiences—and let them provide evidence that you're going to get through *this*. Look to that to remind you that it's possible for something even better to come on the other side of something so tragic.

Whether you find yourself in a "good" season of life or a "bad" one right now, I've learned that it's helpful to realize, or remember, that it *is* a season. And what do seasons do? They pass.

While we've established that we never know what is going to happen in life from one day to the next—or from one moment to the next—that doesn't mean that we live in utter chaos. If you look closely, you will find patterns, just like we can see patterns in the seasons of the year.

The winter is cold and dark. You're grieving the loss of light. Survival is key. It's a time to find refuge. Protect your mental and emotional well-being.

Spring is a time of growth. Set new intentions, focus on what you want to grow, and plant the seeds. Be open to new possibilities. Something new is emerging.

When summer comes, it's time to do the hard work. Not only to keep the new crops growing, but also to fend off weeds and birds and other "predators" that threaten your new growth. Everything is becoming what it is designed to be.

Then comes the fall. There is still hard work to be done, but it's not the hard work of pushing, forcing, or striving. It's the work reaping the harvest of all you've done previously. Your intentions have come to life, and you simply allow abundance to flow.

It took me a long time to recognize and appreciate the pattern of the seasons. I would find myself in the springtime and think, "This is amazing!" Or in the fall and think, "Now we're cooking!" But then that season would end, and I would think, "Damn! I lost it! What did I do wrong?" And I would go into a depression.

When you recognize the pattern, though, when you know there are seasons, then you can flow through them with ease. It doesn't mean that some seasons aren't still more pleasant and desirable—and different seasons come easier to each of us—but you know that whatever is here, it is temporary. When it's unpleasant, this too shall pass. When it's glorious, this too shall pass.

Which season of life does it feel like you're in right now?

Look for evidence of these patterns in your life and let that evidence give you faith that there are possibilities in this moment that you have yet to see.

During the pandemic, rather than thinking, "here we go again," I wrote, "I see my business being even better on the other side of this. I see myself doing work that I love even more than the work that I've loved over the past few years. I believe it. I know it. And this is what pulls me forward."

If you'd like to tap into the power of your story, take a few minutes right now and think about a time where you faced what looked like the end and you got through it, and it was the beginning of something even better in your life. I don't care how far back you have to go to find that experience. You might've been seven years old. That's fine. The whole idea is to find proof that possibility is there.

Whatever you find, add it as evidence in what I call a "faith file." This is what you lean on when circumstances tempt you to worry or to be hopeless. You don't have to take my word for it that you can get through your present—and future—challenges. Take your own word for it.

"This" Is Part of It

There's another benefit to creating your "faith file." If you can string together all the moments of your past and see they've brought you here and that something good has come of it, it means even in those moments when you thought everything was falling apart, there was a purpose. When it seemed nothing was going right, that moment was also a step on the path to now. Somehow, something good was happening even then.

You see, everything belongs. There is nothing wasted. That means that even in this moment, whether you see it or not, something good is happening. This moment is somehow an important link on the chain that gets you to where you want to go, allows you to become who you truly are, to know who you truly are. That means this moment matters.

If you can draw a line—no matter how crooked or winding—through all the points on your journey, from where you started to where you are now, then one thing is definitely true:

every moment on the journey connects together to bring you here. Every moment on the journey is a link in the chain the connects there to here.

What I've learned is that this moment isn't just something to get through, but it's a key step on the journey to get to where you're going. At one point, I could have—and would have—said, "I failed because I don't have a career in music," or, "my marriage failed," or, "my business failed." Now, I know that every one of those low points—as undesirable as they were—were necessary to get me here. Every one of them had a lesson (or lessons) to teach.

On a much smaller scale, I even remember this when I'm preparing for a speaking engagement. Since every talk I do is customized to the audience, I would always come to a point in the preparation process where I would think, "This is going to suck!" It peaked one night years ago when I was getting ready to speak to a medical audience in Delaware.

I was up late into the night revamping my presentation and it just didn't feel right. I had myself scared out of my mind. *I'll just give them their money back if it's horrible*, I thought. I finally went to sleep that night, surrendered to the idea that it was as good as it was going to get.

The next day, I delivered the talk and the client was thrilled. The audience was engaged, we had fun together, and it created something very meaningful for them. Ever since then, I've come to accept, "Oh, *this* is part of it!" I just know that that "messy" part is necessary to get to the final masterpiece. And I tell myself, "Of course it sucks right now. It should suck. It's not finished!"

Now, I don't even worry when I get to that space. "Oh, it's the liminal space again. Here we are." Once again, I'm drawing from evidence in my faith file that tells me it's all going to be fine... and this is part of it.

And when you come to that place, *that's* where you can say, "How grateful I am. Just because."

If we can look back and see that everything we've been through has brought us to this moment, and recognize that despite being pressed and squeezed, we haven't been crushed... If we can acknowledge that we are still here, and say, "Not only am I still here, but I am better (wiser, stronger, more compassionate, more resourceful, whatever it may be) than I was before," then we can redeem the past. We can say, "Yes, the plan is good. I see that now."

And guess what? If we can redeem the past, we can redeem the present. It's not just about acknowledging that everything has been good up to this point and waiting to see what happens next. No. It means if we can see that there has been an undercurrent of grace, of good, maybe even God, up to this point, then we can recognize that there is an undercurrent of the same in this very moment.

See, that's what this is all about. It's not only about making sense of the past, but it's about finding peace and meaning and purpose and joy right here in this very moment, right here as it is.

When you put all of this together—look for signs, reference your faith file, know that this is part of it—then you find the support you need to relax, let go, and trust. What is the ultimate demonstration of trust, though? That's what I was about to learn.

The Power of Surrender

A couple of months after speaking on Sawyer Brown Road, just a couple of nights before Christmas, I was home alone, sitting on the couch, watching TV when there was a knock at my door. I got up and walked over to the door, wondering who was interrupting my rare kid-free night at home. Looking through the peephole, I saw a man with a badge. Probably looking for a kid lost in the apartment complex, I imagined.

When I opened the door, the man said, "Are you Shawn Ellis?"

Okay, so not looking for a lost kid. Unless I was a suspect, but I knew that wasn't the case. I had covered my tracks too well. (Dark humor. Sorry.)

"Yes, I am," I said.

The man handed me a manila envelope filled with a stack of papers. Remember those bill collectors who had been calling? The calls I wasn't answering? Well, what I found out is if you don't answer, they'll eventually come knocking. Just like in life.

Life gives you the little nudges—the hints, the calls, the desires—and we always have the choice to answer or ignore. If you ignore long enough, the avoided calls will eventually come knocking.

As I've admitted, I have a history of being slow and stubborn. On many occasions over the years, I've known what I needed to do long before I actually did it. The calls would come and I would ignore them. Then, life would just keep dialing up the intensity of the adversity, applying just the right amount of pressure to "force" me to push through my fear and do the thing I needed to do, to become the person I needed—and wanted—to become.

It's because of the adversity I've faced that I've had to think long and hard about what really matters to me, what I really want, who I really want to be... and then take the bold steps toward being, doing, or having those things. I believe we are each designed for and called to something bigger than we can possibly imagine. If you're feeling the call to some big and bold moves right now, yet you've been shrinking in fear as I have, here's my advice: Go ahead and make the move now.

It's always easier when you answer the call than when they come knocking, sometimes with a badge. If you still ignore them when they come knocking, by the way, they'll take it up a notch and bust the door down. (That's the health crisis, the broken marriage, the failed business—when you missed all the calls leading up to it that said, "Hey, there's a problem brewing here.")

Life lesson over. Now back to our regularly scheduled programming.

Thankfully, the man with the badge was very kind. He handed me the papers and said, "You've got about three months to figure out how you want to handle this. Otherwise, here's your court date."

Having just recently learned to relax, let go, and trust, I did the natural thing and... tried once again to control the circumstance, to find a way, to make it happen. Like a caged animal stuck in that in-between space, I was scrambling to get out.

I'll find a way to make some money.

I'll go into sales mode.

I tried, but to no avail. I couldn't find a way out.

It seemed that there was only one thing left to do, which was one thing I had avoided for years. One thing I never wanted to do. Which was to declare bankruptcy.

As an entrepreneur, declaring bankruptcy felt even more humiliating than getting a divorce. My identity was wrapped up in the business, and now being more than six figures in debt, unable to dig out, it felt like I had failed. Like I couldn't do it.

Granted, there had been the Great Recession, there had been an adoption, and then a divorce. My spouse hadn't worked since a year-and-a-half into the marriage, so I had carried the weight of our financial wellbeing. And for most of Brody's life, I had been his primary caregiver, taking him to parents' day out and then preschool, and picking him up, finding pockets in between to work.

These were real challenges, but still, I thought I should be able to overcome anything. And clearly, I hadn't. If only I had answered "the calls" that came so often along the way, saying, "this isn't right," but I didn't, and here I was. So, I made a call to a friend of mine who happened to be a bankruptcy attorney and made an appointment to talk with him about my situation.

There was one more challenge I hadn't accounted for. You have to *pay* a bankruptcy attorney. Even though the whole thing is happening because you don't have money. *How am I going to make this work?* I wondered.

Thankfully, I had a small retirement fund from my previous job, so after making an early withdrawal and gathering the necessary info for my attorney—one of the most exhausting processes I've been through—I soon found myself sitting in a courtroom on a snowy Nashville morning doing the thing I never thought I would do.

They don't let you do this in private, by the way. It was me and about 25 other people who had to sit before the judge one person at a time and answer his questions about our situation as he reviewed our documentation. Questions like, for me, "What do you have all these domain names for?" He wondered if I was a domain squatter sitting on thousands of dollars' worth of URLs, but nope, I'm just a guy who runs a business built on ideas.

If you ever think someone who filed for divorce or bankruptcy took "the easy way out," know that they didn't. These are difficult decisions and difficult processes to navigate through.

Here's where things get interesting, though.

Quick note: It was I, not my business, who went bankrupt. I had sacrificed myself financially to keep the business afloat.

That's an important detail because what this meant was that while my personal debt was canceled, there was about 20 thousand dollars in bills to be paid by the business within the next two months. Bankruptcy cancels debt, but it doesn't produce income, so I still didn't know how all of this was going to work out. *How am I going to pay those bills? What about daily living expenses?*

The day I filed bankruptcy, my bank account had $5 in it. With no more credit cards, I was flying without a safety net. And just like the feeling of being caught by the air when I jumped out of the airplane, I was about to experience what it feels like to be caught by the Universe.

"May the floodgates open," I wrote in my journal as a prayer.

I committed to show up, give, and love all I can. Beyond that, "I trust in You (God, Universe, Source)."

And, while I wanted it to all be "fixed" immediately, I leaned on something Hobie—from Sawyer Brown, who, after being one of my childhood heroes, had become one of my dearest friends—had told me: "One foot in front of the other."

That very month—really, that very *week*—everything began to change.

More than $30,000 in new business was verbally confirmed that week, and I received my first international speaking invitation—an engagement with Rotary International for their international conference in Toronto, which would be headlined by Justin Trudeau.

"All according to plan?" I wrote in my journal—with a smiley face.

In the weeks ahead, more bookings came in. Within six weeks, I was able to pay the bills that were due and pay myself a salary for the first time in years. Within three months, we had our best month ever in 15 years in business. And it kept going. A new consulting opportunity. My first half-day workshop.

"I am amazed," I wrote in my journal. "I have nothing but gratitude."

Before the end of that year, we broke that new "best month ever" record—almost doubled it—and by far, it was our best year ever in 15 years in business. So, bankrupt to best year ever... in nine months.

I'd love to say that this is exactly how I imagined it, and that this was a product of my amazing manifesting abilities. The truth is, though, my "realistic expectation"—and hope—was for things to turn around in two, three, or four years. If I could have things stabilized and moving forward by that time, I would have been very happy.

"First you reboot, then you rebuild."

Just as we said that sometimes circumstances linger longer than you expect and change takes longer than you think, sometimes, things turn around much quicker than you would have ever imagined. And I can only point to one reason.

When I sat in the courtroom that day, it was my version of raising the white flag, saying, "Okay, I've gone as far as I can go. I don't know what else to do. I can't figure this out."

In other words, I surrendered. And isn't surrender the ultimate demonstration of trust? If you trust in someone, or something—if you truly trust—then there is no need for you to hold up your defenses in any way. You have full confidence that no matter what, "they've" got you.

I like to picture it like this:

Imagine you're hosting a gathering with friends. Everyone shows up and you ask what they want to eat before placing a delivery order. You order the food, and then what do you do? You resume conversations, playing games in the backyard, or whatever you're doing. Because you know the food is coming.

You don't—I don't imagine—hang up the phone and go sit on the front step watching the street, checking your watch, wondering when or if they will show up. You trust that they will do their job—hopefully—and you just "allow" that they will show up when the food is ready.

That's what trust looks like.

In this case, I didn't know what the Universe had in store for me, but if you believe that God is good, the Universe is good, Life is good, then you do your best and... rest.

And even when you come to a place that doesn't look like anything yet—and even if it looks worse than when it already didn't look like anything yet—you keep going. Because you know that you're doing the right thing, making better choices, and you trust that it's going to work out.

I'm reminded of another lesson I learned from my dear friend and mindfulness teacher, Elmo. He told us the story of a spiritual teacher named Jiddu Krishnamurti who came to San Francisco to deliver a program. During a session, he quietly asked his students, "Do you want to know my secret?" All of the students leaned in to hear his wisdom. Then he revealed his secret: "I don't mind what happens."

Krishnamurti's teachings emphasize the significance of observing life without attachment or aversion, which aligns with the essence of his statement. What if, no matter what situation or circumstances you encountered, you could say sincerely, "I don't mind what happens"? What profound freedom would you experience if you had no attachment to specific outcomes?

But as poetic as that may sound, as enlightened as it may sound, if you want to adopt this belief or this philosophy, expect to be put to the test.

My dear friend, Jeff, once told me, "You know, Shawn, it's always darkest..." As he began, I thought what you're thinking: "just before the dawn." *Got it, Jeff.*

But here's the thing about Jeff. He was not one who would toss out clichés. He was a brilliant speaker and storyteller whose perspective—and humor—I always cherished. It was Jeff who was my partner in creating and conducting the Heart-Centered Speaking Workshop in San Diego.

Another reason "this moment matters" is because you never know when the last time will be the last time. I certainly didn't know that the last time I spoke to Jeff in the Fall of 2020 would be the last time I would speak to him on this earth. He was a casualty of Covid, and I miss him dearly. But, as his wife, Jaffe—a beautiful woman and beautiful soul, herself—said, "He has just relocated."

Jeff didn't have a cliché for me on this day, either. What he said was, "It's always darkest just before... it goes pitch black."

Well played, Jeff. I didn't see that coming.

It did indeed feel like things had gone pitch black, but after it goes pitch black... then comes the dawn.

Thank goodness I kept going when the Universe told me, "Don't worry if it doesn't look like anything yet." Just as I kept painting when Steve Ross said the same. In both cases, the results were better than I could have imagined.

By the end of the painting workshop that day, I looked down at my canvas and saw something that blew me away. A big, majestic mountain. Lots of happy little trees. And that big, hot pink "mess" that had been on my canvas to start became the beautiful sky and reflective water that made the backdrop to accent everything else.

Maybe Bob is right, I thought. *Maybe I can do it after all.*

What if I had given up, though? On that day, or on that journey over the past decade. Believe me, there were plenty of times when I wanted to. Times when I thought, *Maybe speaking isn't for me.* Or when I thought, *maybe it's just time to get a job.*

But every time, something in me said, keep going. I couldn't *not* do it. And so, I did.

I kept painting after the workshop, too. By the end of the year I had done ten paintings, completing the last one on New Year's Eve as a bookend on the year. That painting is my favorite one. I keep my first painting and my last in my office just to remind me what's possible. To remind me to not give up. To keep going.

And I'm sharing all this to remind *you* to keep going, too.

I don't know where you are, or what place you're in right now, but don't worry if it doesn't look like anything yet.

Your best masterpiece has yet to be seen.

Chapter 7

Up We Go

A Dream Delayed Is Not Denied

IF THIS BOOK WERE an episode of *The Joy of Painting* with Bob Ross, this is about the time when Bob would say, "The clock on the wall says I've got a couple minutes left so... let's get crazy, what the heck?!"

Then he would proceed to take what had looked like a "good" painting and risk ruining it by loading up his fan brush with a lot of paint and then... running it right down over the canvas, putting a "great big ole tree" in the middle of it.

Likewise, I could've stopped *Mastering the Moments* with the last chapter and sent you on your way. It would've been a pretty good book, I think, and left you with an idea or two you could apply to make a meaningful difference in your life.

If you're feeling satisfied, you're welcome to close the book and stop reading right here. If you're open to getting a little "crazy," though, there's a little more to the story that I'd love to share with you...

I told you about standing, staring at that END sign. I had no idea, at that moment, that in less than a year our entire world—and my entire world—would change when the global pandemic hit. Truly, there was an "end" up ahead. And, while I couldn't see it as clearly as that wide sandy beach and endless Pacific Ocean, there was also a new beginning to be discovered.

First, I need to tell you about what happened the *day after* I saw that END sign...

While I had Brody with me, I was actually in Los Angeles for a business trip as I mentioned. I had just brought him—with his mom as his travel companion—out a couple days prior for that return to the first place where he had seen the ocean. I was there for a client's event, though—the Future of Work-themed 50th anniversary celebration of Pepperdine University's Graziadio Business School.

One day, a few months before that trip, I had some downtime, so I let myself jump into an internet rabbit hole... as we do.

My fascination with *Knight Rider* and KITT had continued from childhood. While I had "given up" on my prayer for a visit from *Knight Rider*, the nostalgia was still strong. I'm guessing you have some of those things from your childhood that you still love, too.

One thing I learned over the years is that there are shops that build replicas of the KITT car—either you provide a 1980s Pontiac Trans-Am or they do, and they deck it out with all the lights, buttons, screens, and even the voice. No Turbo Boost, unfortunately, but still, pretty cool.

Since I had started telling the "Praying for *Knight Rider*" story in my presentations in 2018, I thought, *You know what? One day,*

I'm going to build one of those and it will be mine. How cool would that be?!

So, on this day, I was reading about the replicas, looking for the nearest shop, checking costs, and so on. While bouncing around from one website to another, I landed on a blog post that mentioned that someone had one of these replicas available for rent in LA. I thought, *Man, I'm going to be in LA in a couple of months!*

And what do you do when life gives you the opportunity? You say YES!

I reached out to the owner and confirmed that it was available on the one "down" day I had in LA. I immediately confirmed the booking for a one-day rental, and then reached out to my friend, Terry, who lives in the area and is an amazing photographer and videographer. "Wanna have some fun?" I asked. He was "in" and the fun was "on"!

The day Brody and his mom left LA for Nashville was the day I would get to drive KITT. I woke up that morning overflowing with excitement and anticipation. Think about waking up for Christmas morning when you were a child and you'll have some idea of what I was feeling.

I called an Uber and the driver took me to the KITT-car owner's home. It was a nondescript neighborhood street. He let me out and I started walking up the driveway. After a few steps, I saw it. That black shiny car. The scanning beacon. Parked right there waiting for me.

The owner came out and proceeded to give me the ins and outs of driving "KITT," pointing out that the speedometer was inaccurate, as was the gas gauge, and informing me that "it's *technically* illegal to turn on the red light while you're driving" since it's not an emergency response vehicle.

Disclaimers out of the way, I was on my way.

I headed out on to the freeway, on my way to a meeting with a brilliant content consultant, Stephanie, before then meeting Terry for some photos and videos. Being the rule follower that I am, I kept the red flashing light turned off—until a van passed me and a preteen boy put down his window and made the universal sign to "turn on the light." Rules be damned, I wasn't going to let his dreams be dashed the way mine were as a kid. I flipped on the light and he gave me a fist pump. It made his day *and* mine.

When I entered Stephanie's neighborhood, I decided to flip on the light once again and wind through the streets in the event that there might be a kid in someone's house who had prayed the same prayer, "Man, it would be amazing to see that car." No kids came running out, but it was worth the effort... and I didn't mind some extra time with KITT.

After finishing my meeting with Stephanie and before going to meet Terry, I decided I better get gas, just to be safe. It was the first of two gas station stops that day, and on both occasions, guys about my age came up and asked to look at the car. Their faces lit up just as brightly as mine. I started it up for them and let them hear the greeting in that oh-so-familiar voice: "This is the voice of Knight Industries Two Thousand. K-I-T-T, or KITT, if you prefer..."

Even for the guy driving his nice, modern Audi A8 sedan, this 30-some-year-old hunk of metal was the cooler vehicle. He came over and told me how he loved that car as a kid, too. "Yeah, my son doesn't get it," he said.

Ugh. Kids these days.

My dad asked me later, "Did it have any special features?"

"Nope," I told him. No oil slicks, no Turbo Boost, nothing like that. And on top of it, the USB port on the aftermarket stereo—hidden away under the custom dash—also didn't have much juice to recharge a cell phone. So, recognizing that my phone was going to die before I got the car back to its home later that evening, I pulled over and wrote down the directions by hand on the back of an envelope in my bag.

Still, I was driving KITT, and it was amazing.

I took a selfie sitting in the car, with a big smile on my face at one point. If you were to ask me, "Hey Shawn, what are you thinking about?" It would have been an easy answer: "Driving KITT!"

As my business was turning around in 2018, I came across a question: "How can it get even better than this?" It's another tool to keep pulling you toward possibilities. In the midst of my best year ever, it was hard to imagine something even better. But this was even better.

When I was a kid, I thought a visit from *Knight Rider* would be the best. Just to see it parked in my driveway, and maybe to have a chance to sit inside it. That's all I wanted. That was the best I could imagine. And I was crushed when it didn't happen.

I never imagined that 35 years later, not only could I see the car and sit in it, but I could drive the damn thing! I had no idea *that* was a possibility. And after all the build-up, and all the lessons I learned along the way, the experience was so much more rewarding than if I had just sat in it for a few minutes as a kid.

Prior to driving KITT, I spent years wondering, "What did I do wrong?" with my *Knight Rider* prayer—and with so many other "unanswered" prayers in my life. After the experience of driving KITT, though, it's given me an entirely different perspective.

Ralph Waldo Emerson said, "When you make a decision, the Universe conspires to make it happen." That makes me think: What if, when I prayed that prayer at age seven, my prayer was answered in that moment? What if the Universe cued up the experience at that time, but then it just took me 35 years to become the person who was ready to fully embrace it?

The journey of *Mastering the Moments* leads you to look at life differently.

For example, now I wonder, what if *Knight Rider* had come on that day when I was seven? It would have been a thrill, for sure, but maybe it would have also given me the idea that you can have anything you want, anytime you want it. And that's not how life works.

As much turmoil as it caused me over the years wondering "what did I do wrong?" with my *Knight Rider* prayer, how much more turmoil might it have caused if I went through the rest of my life wondering why all my *other* prayers weren't being answered just like my *Knight Rider* prayer?

Some of the "microwave miracles"—as I call them—that we ask for are requested with the best of intentions, but with a lack of ability to see the bigger picture. The healing of a loved one, for example, would be great... but what about when the next illness comes? Or the next? At some point, death—as humans—is inevitable.

We could say the same of requests for relationship break-throughs, financial breakthroughs, career breakthroughs, and the list goes on. Fixing *this* "problem" doesn't make you immune to future ones.

We are driven to avoid pain and pursue pleasure, and our prayers—or wishes, or visions, or goals—reflect that. Life includes pain *and* pleasure, though. The fullness of the human experience includes *all* of it.

Just because we don't get *what* we want—or what we think we want—*when* we want it doesn't mean that our prayer hasn't been answered. It just means that for whatever reason, it hasn't been answered—or delivered—*yet*.

What if, even when it appears as if your requests are being ignored, or that your manifesting powers have run dry, you could know the Universe really *is* on your side, and has been the entire time? What if you could believe the entire system is rigged in your favor? How would it shape your experience from one moment to the next if you lived in that truth?

Nothing says what you want will happen immediately, or that what you want will show up exactly the way you expect. Sometimes, what we want isn't even what we really need. But when we trust that the Universe is on our side, we can embrace *whatever* comes, knowing it can lead to something truly extraordinary.

Where Is the Joy?

In late 2019, the year after my "best year ever," things were humming along. I had driven KITT. I had taken Brody to Yellowstone. I had more speaking opportunities than ever before. I was building the team. And we were working to build on the momentum of the past year.

At one point, I was traveling to a new event every week for six weeks straight. If you had asked me when I started speaking what I wanted, this would have been it. I had two brilliant women on my team, and we were developing a new Built to Thrive coaching program for organizations.

The final event of the six-week run was a small event for Bridgestone in Nashville. It was a Tuesday. I remember seeing their headquarters—a 30-floor tower—being built in Nashville, so it was especially exciting to get to speak there. I went in and gave them my best. That night, though, I melted into my couch. My tank was empty.

You know that feeling when you've pressed hard to get through a tough season—maybe it was a move, maybe it was a class, maybe it was a season of travel baseball, maybe it was publishing a book—and then when you can finally exhale, you are just *done*? You've been running on adrenaline, and now the pressure is off... and you didn't realize just how exhausted you really were.

That was me.

While I was sitting there, an alert popped up on my phone. A friend, Keisha—an astrologist and tarot card reader I had met in a virtual mastermind group—was doing her free "Tarot Tuesday" event on Facebook Live. She would draw a card and do a complimentary reading for anyone who wanted.

I had been curious about tarot readings, but I had never done one. Now, I clearly wasn't getting off my couch, so, why not? I entered the chat and said I'd like her to draw a card for me.

I waited. Person after person had their reading. Maybe she had missed me, so I commented again that I'd like a reading. This time, she acknowledged my request, and a few minutes later, it was my turn.

I'll just tell you; I was expecting this to be something like a fortune cookie. "Good things are coming your way." "Hang in there." "The future looks bright for you." Something like that—a non-specific, positive, encouraging word. That's why I was shocked when she pulled my card and held it up to the camera. The best way I can describe is to say it looked like Edvard Munch's painting, The Scream. *What the hell?* I thought.

The first thing Keisha said was, "Don't worry."

Hahaha. She knew. That was scary AF.

Then she went on, "What I see here is stress, stress, stress."

Okay, this was not going to be a generic fortune cookie message.

She continued, "If there's something you've been working on, maybe you just need to shelve it for a minute. Breathe. Trust your God or your Source."

Turns out, that was just the message I needed to hear. She said the words that I had been feeling in my soul. When there is alignment, you feel it, and this felt like total alignment.

The next morning, I told my team we needed to pause the projects for a moment. Having looked at the business records and the bank accounts, I saw that we didn't *have* to force anything, and Keisha's reading was right, I needed to catch my breath.

The next weekend, I had tickets to attend a couple of one-day workshops for my own growth, and I did. Both placed a heavy emphasis on meditation, which had been getting squeezed out of my life in the recent busy-ness. Over the weekend, I spent probably five hours total in meditation. I took time to reflect and journal, and during that time, a question came to me:

Where is the joy?

I told you about how, at one point, all I wanted was peace.

But also, remember when I saw that smile on Brody's face, and I told you it was pure joy? And how, what we all want is that joy? *The Joy of Painting. The Joy of Cooking. The Joy of Sex.* We are looking for the *joy*. The *fullness* of life.

Just a year after learning the powerful lesson about surrender, I was back to pushing again. I was doing work I loved, working with people I loved, and yet, the joy had been squeezed out. Have you ever experienced that?

As I said, at one point, my present life was my dream. You don't know what your dream feels like until you experience it, though, and when I experienced it, it wasn't everything I thought it would be.

After more time contemplating that question, *where is the joy?* I came up with this answer in my journal:

I am a voice for those who feel overwhelmed, discouraged... lost...

My mission is to provide a place of refuge—to show them that refuge is available right here, now, in this moment.

Not only is refuge available in this moment, but something more...

You can RISE in this moment.

There is magic in this moment, if you are open to it.

That's where the joy is.

And you might think, *Shawn, you're weird.* And we've established that—I am.

For you, the joy might be on a golf course or sitting on a white sandy beach. For you, the joy might be in playing Lego's with your kids or cooking in the kitchen.

For me, though, as I shared before, coming alongside people in times of difficulty—offering whatever I can offer to lighten their load—lights me up.

As I read back over what I wrote, I realized: There is no mention of my vocation. It doesn't say anything about writing or speaking or coaching or teaching. It hit me; I can do this anywhere. I can show up making copies at the office—nod to the old Rob Schneider skit on *Saturday Night Live*—and I can fulfill this mission. I can mop floors and fulfill this mission.

Then I thought, if I can do this anywhere, I better start at home. With my family. Let me be a place of refuge for *them*.

Where is the joy?

When you find what truly lights you up, and when there's no attachment to any specific thing that has to happen in order for you to do it, then you have freedom.

I wrote later in my journal, as I reset my intentions for the year ahead, "I am home more than I am away."

This was 2019, remember? Apparently, my manifesting powers are stronger than I realized. I'm sorry?

As I settled back into this place of aligning and allowing, rather than hustling and grinding, wouldn't you know, we went on to have our best month of the year.

Truly, there is magic in this moment, if you are open to it.

And this is the journey. There is no arriving. There is no "there." There is just a continuous, upward spiral toward becoming who you truly desire to be—and more than that, who you truly *are*. It is an upward spiral of learning, growing, and rising higher and higher in our understanding and experience of life. And every moment is part of that journey.

While years ago, I only longed for peace—a state of calm and contentment amidst the chaos—now I understand that true peace also includes something more—*joy*. I first saw it in Brody's smile when he was riding his bike, I felt it while I was driving KITT, and now I know it is the active, vibrant expression of life that calls to us all. It is the spark that lights up our lives and gives meaning to our experiences.

Like peace, joy can only be experienced in the present moment. And true joy, I've discovered, comes from two things: being in service to others, and embracing growth. As a matter of fact, when seeking the answer to that ever-present question, "What is the right thing, right now?" there are two questions that bring further clarity:

What is the path to my greatest growth?
What is the path to serving at the highest level?

Both of those questions will surely take you outside of your comfort zone, and initially, that doesn't feel like peace. But they will pull you forward and invite you to engage fully with life… and when you do that, you will find a joy *and* a peace like you've never felt.

In times of disruption, discouragement, and even depression, peace may be the thing that calls to you. Follow it. But never allow yourself to go too long without asking the question, "Where is the joy?" lest you sink back into the complacency of survival mode. Do not mistake the stillness of complacency for peace.

You might say that peace grounds us, while joy elevates us. Together, they create a life of meaning and purpose.

We all need the vitality and enthusiasm that joy brings. Joy is found in the active pursuit of our passions, in our connection to others, and in the contributions we offer to the world. It comes from serving others and growing beyond our perceived limitations.

When we embrace and commit to all of this, *then* we are *Mastering the Moments*, living our true calling, moving higher and higher on the spiral of life. When we understand that "this is the way," then we can know that in every ending, there is a new beginning, and in the space in between, there is a path to peace and a path to joy.

In the years since, the question "Where is the joy?" has led me to embrace new experiences and make significant life changes, both big and small.

For instance, I bought tickets to see Garth Brooks—one of my "bucket list" items—which, both as a spectator and a musician, was an absolute thrill. I had to press through the discomfort of going by myself, though, doing it purely because I wanted to and because I could.

As it turns out, I may have been there as a gift to the husband of the woman seated next to me. I say that because she told me all about her love for Garth Brooks while he, according to her, was not so enthusiastic. He was able to keep up with his email while I provided a listening ear for his wife. So, I had the joy of growing and serving all at once!

More seriously, reflecting on "What is the path to my greatest growth?" and "What is the path to serving at the highest level?" has also driven me to make big moves. For example, these questions prompted my move from Tennessee to Ohio, putting Brody in a much better learning environment and allowing us both to be closer to family.

Professionally, those questions inspired me to re-envision my speaking presentations and reshape The Speakers Group into a true community of speakers, all united by a mission to help people live better lives and build better businesses. The drive to do "work I believe in" has remained, but now my life is about so much more than just work.

These guiding questions have also led me to reevaluate my relationships. I stopped dating women I felt "comfortable" with and opened myself to connections that challenged and excited me. This led me to find an amazing, brilliant, hilarious, and sexy woman, Megan—who is also the mother of two incredible kids of her own—who I didn't even know I was looking for. Now, I am grateful to wake up every day with a true partner on this journey, walking each other home.

Side note, it was our shared belief in and love for "signs" like 11:11 that initially connected us and continues to remind us to "relax, let go, and trust" as we navigate life together—although there's not a lot of "relaxing" in a home with three kids.

And, purely by chance—or was it?—we got engaged on the 23rd of February. That just happened to be the day I got the call that the ring was ready, and I couldn't wait to propose.

You see, it all belongs, and *this* is part of it. The journey is certainly not linear. It's an upward spiral. And we move through it one moment at a time, one foot in front of the other.

I don't know what lies ahead for me or for you, but whatever it is, I'll leave you with one last story and lesson from My Little Guru...

Something Awesome Is About to Happen

The year Brody and I moved into our two-bedroom apartment—which I knew was the "right thing, right now," but which also scared me, for him and for me—I was in that space between an ending and a beginning. Clearly, we weren't where we used to be, and I hoped—and believed—for the best... but I didn't know how it would all go.

I was worried about him. Not only did I never want to divorce, I also certainly didn't want to put my child through that. I know that causes trauma. And yet, so does staying in an unhealthy environment. As it often is in life, the "right" path is rarely, if ever "easy."

They say kids are resilient, and on this day, I got a glimpse of it.

It was just about a month after we had moved out of our house when I heard four-year-old Brody say to his "kitty" (actually a blanket, but it was a "kitty" to him for as long as I can remember), "Something awesome is going to happen."

"What's going to be awesome?" I asked him.

"I don't know," he said. "Just wait."

Dammit. My Little Guru.

Was that simply a demonstration of the resilience of a child? Or was that the Universe telling *me*, something awesome is about to happen?

What if I—and we—adopted the same belief, that in any given moment, something awesome is going to happen? No telling what it will be, or when it will happen, but you just have to wait for it, expect it, and be on the lookout.

Just like, while driving KITT on that Spring Day in 2019, I had no idea that the whole world—and my whole world—would be turned upside down in less than a year, right now, I have no idea what's up ahead. I can't even imagine what's possible—and that goes for the "good" and the "bad."

While I'm still prone to get anxious and worry and fear the worst amid all the uncertainty, ultimately, I come back to what I know. And what I know is:

Something awesome is going to happen.

No doubt about it.

And not only that, I believe something awesome is *happening*, right now.

Even if what you see is that something you know and love is ending.

Even if it feels like you're starting over.

Even if it feels like you've hit a wall.

This ending will give way to a new beginning. And while it feels like you're starting over, you're not. Because you still have everything you've learned so far. You're not the same person you were at the beginning.

What looks like a wall—when you zoom out—is actually a step and an invitation to rise up to the next level.

At that point, God, the Universe, Life, extends a hand and says, "Come on! Up we go!"

I'm honored and grateful to be on the journey with you.

Acknowledgements

In my journal on January 20, 2015, I noted these words from Wayne Dyer: "Open up to receiving the assistance you desire. Stay alert, and be willing to accept any guidance that comes your way." I have received so much assistance and guidance during my lifetime—some of which is captured within the pages of this book, but even more is not.

I believe we are all connected, part of one universal body and mind. Somehow, through our connection, we "call" one another into our lives at just the perfect moments in time. Some of these *intersections*, as I call them, last for moments, some for seasons, and some for lifetimes. As Ram Dass says, "We're all just walking each other home."

This book is very much a collection of stories of intersections during that walk. While I'm grateful for all of them, there are some individuals whose influence has been especially meaningful, and it brings me joy to acknowledge them here.

First, I thank my parents, John and Carolyn, for supporting my wild dreams every step of the way. Mom, you calmly listened to my worries and fears and inspired me to keep going. Dad, I still have the songbook you signed to "My country rock star son." Turns out, it was your old Nightingale-Conant tape sets rather than the country albums that were more closely aligned with my path. Neither of us would have guessed I would end up following the motivational speakers on those tapes rather than the artists on the records! To both of you, my story is an extension of your story.

To my brother, Kirk, thank you for always listening patiently as I've shared stories of my life's latest twists and turns, and for sharing your stable, grounded perspective in return. Our brotherhood and friendship has been—and is—a gift to me.

To my grandparents—Grandma and Grandpa, MaMa and PaPa, Granddad and Granny Grace—you each made a meaningful impact on my life and I miss you daily. Your legacy continues through these pages.

To my team members, past and present, you have kept The Speakers Group going for over 20 years. I'm especially grateful to Dawn, who has expertly managed our event logistics for over 15 years and who brings a sense of peace to both me and our clients. And to Jan, who has believed in me and pushed for this book from day one. Jan, your passion and perseverance inspire me more than you know.

To our clients, thank you for giving us the opportunity to help bring your event visions to life. Whether you've invited me to speak or allowed us to help you find and secure another amazing speaker, I don't take that for granted. Your trust in us has been the foundation of our success.

To the speakers I've had the privilege to work with, I have tremendous respect and appreciation for the work you do. I'm honored and humbled to stand alongside you. While there are more speakers than I can name, I have to give a shout-out to Diane Sieg, Mike Marchev, John Livesay, Mike Robbins,

Mike Lee, Mike Evans, Jason Barger, Victoria Labalme, Erik Wahl, Byrd Baggett, Carol Grace Anderson, Harry Paul, Kathy Cleveland Bull, Robert Thompson, Derrick Moore, Neil Rackham, Allan Karl, Chip Eichelberger, Joel Zeff, Joseph Michelli, Vicki Hitzges, Robert Spector, Dan Lier, Dennis Snow, Waldo Waldman, Andy Andrews, and Ron Minatrea. Your support and camaraderie have been invaluable.

To Duane Ward, founder of Premiere Speakers Bureau, who took a chance on me as a 22-year-old shy kid and introduced me to this crazy world of speaking. Duane, you gave me the opportunity to build the corporate speakers division and introduced me to the world of entrepreneurship. I learned more about marketing while working with you than I ever did in college. Your mentorship and ongoing support have had a lasting impact on my career, and I hold deep respect and appreciation for you.

To Scott Crain and Brian Lord, my fellow original members of the Penny Dreadfuls writing group, thank you for your friendship and support—including reading some of my silly submissions back in the day. Know that I've thought of you often throughout this writing process. You inspire me.

To Stephanie DeMizio Kelly, thank you for helping me see the value in my own story. And thank you for generously sharing your brilliant expertise and wisdom over the years so that I could craft this story into something meaningful for readers and audiences. I have no doubt that our "chance" meeting was not by chance.

To M.C. Calvi, thank you for the perspective you've brought to this book. Thank you for helping me not ramble. At least, not as much!

Thank you to great teachers like Tony Robbins, Wayne Dyer, Jon Kabat-Zinn, Brené Brown, Elizabeth Gilbert, Jack Kornfield, Martha Beck, Rob Bell, Ernest Holmes, Henri Nouwen, and many more whose wisdom came to me at just the right time, often through their books. I hope I can share the same gift with others that you have shared with me.

To Hobie, my childhood hero turned dear friend. Your encouragement to "put one foot in front of the other" came at the perfect moment and continues to guide me. Thank you for always asking, "How are YOU doing?"

To Jonathan, the best therapist in Nashville—if you ask me—who helped me see and understand myself when I felt lost. Your wisdom still speaks to me today.

To Brody, My Little Guru, and most importantly, my son. You have taught me so much and continue to teach me every day. I am honored to be your dad and look forward to watching your life unfold. While I was inspired by the idea of *you* being proud of *me*, know that *I* am proud of *you*. You are an amazing young man. Wherever life leads, know that I will always be in your corner, cheering you on.

And to Megan. I'm writing this while sitting across from you, hoping you don't see the tears welling up in my eyes. I had no idea that the hunch to "just see what's out there" would lead me to a woman like you. I am filled with gratitude. Thank you for seeing the best in me and challenging me to live my truth daily. Thank you for loving me even on the days I don't. It's no coincidence that this book, after being in the works for years, has finally come to fruition after meeting you. Not only have you pushed me and encouraged me to get it done, but you've also made tremendous sacrifices to make that possible. I see you, and I appreciate you. You, Caleb, and AJ have changed my—and Brody's—life forever and I am beyond grateful for the life we are building together. Up we go.

Lastly, thank you to you, the reader, for letting me share these stories with you. I hope one day I'll have the chance to hear yours, too. We are all just walking each other home.

About the Author

SHAWN ELLIS is a motivational keynote speaker, dynamic storyteller, and modern-day philosopher. With over 20 years of leadership and entrepreneurial experience, Shawn guides leaders and teams toward adaptability and resilience using insights from mindfulness, neuro- science, and psychology.

Shawn's keynotes and workshops, such as "Mastering the Moments," "Beyond Resilience," and "Adapt & Thrive," empower audiences to navigate life's challenges with grace and strength. He also advises companies on creating resilient cultures that are Built to Thrive. His clients include CMT, Bridgestone, Dippin' Dots, Freddie Mac, and the Cayman Islands Civil Service College.

In addition to speaking and consulting, Shawn is creator of the Rock the Reboot online workshop and host of The Better Life Better Business Podcast. Shawn lives with his family outside Columbus, Ohio.

Sign up for Shawn's weekly email updates at ShawnEllis.com.

CONTINUE YOUR JOURNEY OF
MASTERING THE MOMENTS

Facing a "reboot" in your life and not sure where to go from here? *Rock the Reboot* is an inspiring, engaging, science-backed course with four hours of video-training from Shawn, plus a 91-page "Reboot Playbook" designed to help you rise above adversity and come back better than EVER.

Learn more and enroll at
www.shawnellis.com/reboot

Use promo code *mtmbook*
for a 50% discount on tuition

www.ingramcontent.com/pod-product-compliance
Lightning Source LLC
Chambersburg PA
CBHW011237120626
46549CB00009B/3309